YAKUSHIMA:
A YAKUMONKEY GUIDE

By Clive Witham

SECOND EDITION

© Clive Witham 2013

The right of Clive Witham to be identified as the author of this work has been asserted to him in accordance with the Copyright, Designs and Patents Act 1998

ISBN: 978-0-9561507-1-4

Illustrations © Clive Witham

Published in 2013 by Siesta Press, Dorset, UK

CONTENTS

INTRODUCTION

Four years on from writing the first edition and it is time to assess the changes time has brought to Yakushima. So what has changed?

Well everything……and yet nothing.

The forests are still filled with the same ancient cedar trees so astonishingly old that they were saplings at the birth of the Roman Empire. It still rains heavily high in the mountains creating spectacular waterfalls and crystal clear water so clean it is drinkable straight from source. Wild macaques and deer still roam the mountains in large numbers as they have done for millennia. Species so rare that they only live wild on Yakushima and nowhere else on the planet. But Yakushima is more than any one sight or any one natural phenomena, it is a living, breathing island so full of life that to walk its trails, to touch its greenery and to breathe its air is an affirmation of nature and our place within it. There is nowhere quite like it in the world and its status as a Japanese National Park and a World Natural World Heritage site reflects this rare beauty.

There have been a few changes since the first book. The strain of tourists on some of the trails has been officially acknowledged and now a permanent system of control has been set up for the Arakawa trail entrance and the road leading to it. The portable toilet experiment is no longer an experiment and toilet facilities are now on some of the busiest trails. Fast food arrived in the form of Mossburger, a Japanese hamburger chain, in Anbo and Wi-Fi/internet facilities have been gradually appearing in accommodation and cafes. It would appear that the 21st century has finally made it to Yakushima. Appearances can however be deceptive.

You will find that for the majority of people who live on Yakushima, life is how it always was. The internet is some mysterious contraption that is as far away from them as the coast of mainland Japan. For most life is about people and community. And that it the charm. When you visit Yakushima it is almost like being in a time warp in the days before the technological revolutions most of us take for granted.

This guide is based on my personal knowledge of Yakushima, having lived and worked there both as a fisherman and a wood craftsman. This allows me to draw on a little local knowledge to let you get the best out of visiting and you will find stories and anecdotes throughout the guide book, some of which are mine and some of which are from the wonderful people who live there.

Be aware that this is one of the least wealthy areas of Japan. Nowadays tourism is the island's largest economy with an estimated income of 10 billion yen a year but unfortunately the wealth of mainland tourists has not filtered down to the native islanders. With average incomes still at ¥3 million a year (70% of the national average) and average hourly pay at just ¥650 an hour, many people struggle to make a living. I have therefore tried to include as many local businesses as I could when making this guide and urge you to use smaller Yakushima-based businesses during your stay. Some of these speak little English (those that do I indicate in the guide) but Yakushima is generally a friendly place willing to help and with good humour and persistence most things can be accomplished. Should you need a little help with your Japanese, however, I have included the Japanese words in their original form to aid in communication (you can point to the word!) and to enable you to read signs.

Please note that any businesses marked with ☺ are used to having foreign guests and speak some English. If you are unfamiliar with Japan or speak no Japanese, try these first.

At the risk of stating the obvious the symbols used on the hiking maps are as follows:

🏠 Covered rest area   💧 Water source   🚻 Toilets   🅿 Parking area

For reasons of space I have omitted the prefix (0997) for Yakushima phone numbers so please remember to add this to all local six digit numbers when calling from outside the island.

The hiking details in this guide include all the main trails. There are many other paths dotted around the island, some of which I refer to in this book, but for the sake of the forest I have not included them in this guide. All of the hiking times I have included are estimates and based on a fairly fit person carrying a backpack, please be on the conservative side when planning routes and take account of gradient and weather conditions in conjunction with a proper hiking map. I recommend that instead of pushing on huge distances in one day that you take your time amongst the trees and open your senses to the forest. It is too special a place to rush through. I hope these pages help you to enjoy the wonders of Yakushima.

Clive Witham

Visit yakumonkey.com for updates on visiting Yakushima

1 THE BASICS

Yakushima is 60 km south of Kyushu Island and at the northern end of the Ryukyu island chain that lead on to Okinawa. On a clear day especially after rain has fallen around the coast, the mountains that make up Cape Sata, the furthest point of mainland Kyushu, are clearly outlined on the northern horizon.

Across the Vincennes Strait to the East is Tanegashima (種子島), a relatively flat island, home to Japan's Space exploration program. And to the North West a small volcanic island, only 12 km away, known as Kuchierabu (口永良部島), and which last erupted in 1980.

Visually the island is impressive. There are over 45 mountain peaks squeezed into a total area of 505 km² which makes it look, at least from the sea, like a botanical castle floating in a Miyazaki animation. The mountain ranges are high with the highest peak on the island,

Miyanoura dake rising to 1935 m, making it the tallest mountain in all of southern Japan.

The average altitude of the island is 600 m and as most of it is sloping downwards, there are very few places where the land is completely flat. If you stand at the coast and look inwards to the mountains, they appear to form a massive impenetrable wall all the way round its 132 km circumference.

The island was formed around 14 million years ago when granite base-rock was forced up by seismic activity, a process which has never really halted, and it is still rising at a rate of one meter per 1,000 years. While there is some sandstone and shale at the foot of the central mountains, Yakushima is essentially one giant lump of granite.

Hard and solid granite rocks weather slowly and only produce a small amount of soil, and in theory would not be an ideal environment for plants to thrive, but just a glimpse of any photo of the island will tell you that in Yakushima it is quite the opposite.

THE UNIQUE FLORA

Virtually the whole island is covered in plant life with the state forestry owning a massive 95.5% of Yakushima. And it is here, within the green canopy that covers

Yakushima's mountains, that the unique qualities of the island really come to bear.

A remarkable variety of plants inhabit the island. There are more than 1,900 species and subspecies distributed gradually up the mountain slopes. There are sub-tropical plants, such as banyan trees near the coast, and then a little higher, warm temperate plants such as chinquapin and evergreen oaks. These then give way to temperate zone plants, such as fir and cypress trees as the mountains rise and ultimately as the tree-line is passed to sub alpine plants such as the Yakushima dwarf bamboo and the famous Yakushima rhododendron. According to UNESCO, the range of vegetation across the island from the coast to the high altitude summits is considered to be the widest not only in Japan but in the whole of East Asia.

This unique forest ecosystem in Yakushima is positioned at the extreme end of the natural distribution of many species. It has over 200 species that are at their southern limit of natural distribution, and equally many identified species that are at their very northernmost point. Yakushima acts as a melting pot between northern and southern species allowing an environment where the two can successfully co-exist and unsurprisingly this has resulted in 94 endemic species only found on the island. With a permanently damp micro-climate, it is also home to an astonishing 300 species of fern and 600 varieties of mosses.

As if this was not enough, there is a particular native species considered so rare that it has been awarded 'Special Natural Monument' status in Japan and which has come to symbolize the natural importance of the island. These are the Japanese cedar trees known as 'Yakusugi', each over 1,000 years of age, and found somewhere between 600 m and 1800 m on the mountain slopes. They are very large evergreen trees with a dark reddish brown bark and although often referred to as 'cedar' trees in English, 'Sugi' (*Crytomeria japonica*) actually belong to the cypress family of trees. The wood has a slight red tinge to it, gives off a very distinctive scent and is renowned for its strength and water resistance.

Indeed it was this point that caused them, until very recently, to be almost logged out of existence.

THE FOREST

The cedar forests of Yakushima have a long history of being plundered for the needs of an ever growing Japan. The first records date back to the middle ages when, in the 16th century, forestry surveys of the island were made on the orders of **Hideyoshi Toyotomi** (1537-1598), the great fuedal lord and unifier of Japan, who had an eye on using yakusugi timber in the construction of the Colossal Hall of the Great Buddha of Hokoji Temple in Higashiyama, Kyoto in 1586. In the end it was never used for the temple but it was used in many other structures, including Osumi Sho-hachimangu Shrine (which is now Kagoshima Shrine).

During the Edo period (1603-1868), and under the watchful eye of an eager **Lord Shimazu**, of the powerful Satsuma clan in Kyushu, the cutting was very selective and only relatively straight standing trees began. It is said that **Jochiku Tomari** (泊如竹) (1570-1655), a Confucuianist scholar born in Anbo, had suggested the idea to Shimazu personally and had then persuaded a reluctant island population to agree to cutting down their sacred forests.

Edo period logging

The attraction of yakusugi was that it was both strong and waterproof, making it perfect material to produce the short rectangular roof tiles needed for construction throughout Japan. Each tile had to be 50 cm long, 10 cm wide and 7 mm thick and became the currency of the island's annual tribute to the Satsuma clan. The demand was great in the markets of Osaka and the logging was so intensive that it is believed that over half of the

Yakusugi trees were felled and that only around 1,000 long-lived Yakusugi were left standing.

Evidence of Edo period logging activities is all around when wandering through the forests even today. The path leading up from Kusugawa village known as the Kusugawa trail was originally laid for Edo period forest labourers who had to live and work in the forests for extended periods of time, using simple axes to fell the giant cedars. It was sometimes only after the tree had been cut down that it was decided whether or not to use its wood and many great trees still lay fallen, untouched and still intact on the forest floor.

It was not until the Meiji period (1868-1912) that the first signs of de facto conservation were seen when in 1885 the island's forests were placed into the possession of the state. Despite a long legal battle started in 1904 by Yakushima islanders who saw their forestry livelihood under threat, the state owned forest was confirmed in 1920 and the modern era of logging began.

The first conservation measure was the designation of an Academic Reference Forest Reserve in the national forest and in 1924 it became a Heritage Area known as the 'Yakushima Old Growth Japanese Cedar Forest Natural Monument' (the designation was changed to Special Natural Monument in 1954).

However, despite the rudimentary attempts at protection, logging was well underway. In 1923 the forest path from Anbo to Kosugidani was completed and District Forestry offices set up. By the late 1950s, there was a movement to increase the logging of national parks throughout Japan to ease the demand for building materials in post war reconstruction. Logging was therefore extended to the broad leaved forest as well as the Yakusugi and operations intensified considerably especially after the introduction of the chain saw in 1956.

The trees were brought swiftly down the mountains on one of four forest rail tracks. Only one survives today (from Anbo) and is the only active logging rail track in all of Japan. Pictures in Yakusugi museum show forest workers perched on top of several trunks strapped to an engine-less wagon and with controls not unlike the reins of horse, hurtling down the mountain. Not a job for the faint of heart. Nowadays the trucks have engines and can often be seen at the logging station at Arakawa Trail Entrance.

Further signs of conservation came again in 1964 when the area was incorporated into the **Yaku-Kirishima National Park** (霧島国立公園), but logging continued until national forestry priorities began to change from production to more progressive ideas of development and conservation in the 1960s and it was finally halted as recently as in 1971. It then swiftly became an official Wilderness Area and in the 1980s the national park was

expanded with 19,000 hectares declared a Biosphere Reserve under the UNESCO Man and Biosphere Program. More protection then came with the creation of The Forest Ecosystem Reserve in 1991 and in December 1993 the awarding of **UNESCO World Natural Heritage Site** to Yakushima brought 10,747 hectares of the 50,000 hectares of the total area of Yakushima (21%) under international protection.

This collection of protected areas effectively means that activities which may threaten the 'integrity' of the area, such as building, felling trees or bamboo, collecting animals and plants, collecting soil, stones, rocks, fallen leaves and branches, and building fires are prohibited within the Wilderness Area and allowed only under permit in the Special Protection zone of the National Park and Preservation zone of the National Forest.

More recently, coastal areas have finally come under international protection with Nagata beach designated a **Wetland of International Importance under the Ramsar Convention** in 2005 in recognition of its unique position in the nesting of loggerhead turtles.

Management of the World Heritage area is split between the Environment Agency, the Forestry agency, the Agency for Cultural Affairs and Kagoshima Prefecture. To try to simplify working together the Yakushima World Heritage Area Liaison Committee was formed between them but in reality the problems that Yakushima now faces are exacerbated by a lack of unified administrative control. The sheer numbers of visitors to Yakushima have put a major strain on the island's eco-system with soil erosion and waste management at the forefront.

So far there have been signs that something is being done against the onslaught of tourists on the forests: access to the Arakawa Trail head has now been permanently restricted to private cars and a new system of bio-toilets have been set up. A taskforce was set up in 2012 to look at how to charge visitors at their point of entry. However because there are so many organisations which have to agree before being implemented, change is slow.

The protection of Yakushima is chronically underfunded on a national level and essentially relies on the volunteer work of local people, many of whom neither have the time nor resources to make an effective impact. It is now a fairly regular annual task for locals to climb up to the toilets at Takatsuka mountain hut and carry the contents of the pit latrines down the mountain. Toilets are a major issue as demand exceeds supply and subsequent contamination from pit toilets is causing environmental damage in the areas most needed of protection.

There are further problems in that the mountain huts become so congested in high season that hikers are forced to erect tents around the site, damaging the fragile eco-system. It has been suggested that tourist numbers should be controlled and path closures and other measures need to be implemented to protect the island but, under the current system of management, it appears that change will be very slow.

THE TREES

JOMON SUGI (縄 文 杉)

Height: 25.3m

Diameter: 5.22m

Trunk circumference: 16.4m

Age: 2600-7200 years old

Access: The Okabu trail

The grand daddy of them all. It was probably due to its rough and weathered exterior that it managed to survive the logging activities of the Edo period. It was called Oiwa sugi (大岩杉) up until 1966 when a local man named Teiji Iwakawa (岩川貞 次) bought it national attention. It was then renamed 'Jomon sugi' because initial tests dated it back to the Jomon era (14,000 - 400 BC) and also the fact that the branches appeared to have a similar shape to traditional Jomon earthenware. On its weather beaten, leathery trunk 13 different species of plant life grow, including rhododendron, trochodendron and mountain ash.

YAYOI SUGI (弥生杉)

Height: 26.1 m

Trunk circumference: 8.1 m

Age: 3,000 years old

Access: Shiratani Unsuikyo

The name of this grand old Yakusugi gives us clues about its age. The Yayoi period in Japanese history was between 500 BC and 300 AD and directly followed the Jomon period. It has an odd shape which probably saved it from being felled by Edo period loggers. It is much lower in altitude than many of the other old Yakusugi trees standing at just 710 m above Miyanoura village and common to many of the great Yakusugi, it has ten different epiphyte species

growing from the surface of its trunk including Yakushima Rhododendron, Japanese Rowan and Japan Wood-oil.

BUDDHA SUGI (仏陀杉)

Height: 21.5 m

Trunk circumference: 8.0 m

Age: 1,800 years old

Access: Yakusugiland

This famous Yakusugi has a clump on its trunk which when seen from a certain angle is supposed to resemble to face of Buddha. It is very weak at its lower trunk with much of it hollow and visitors are restricted by the viewing platform 2 m from the tree for its protection.

This has stood since 1997 when attempts to save the tree were put in place including improving soil quality, draining excess water and restricting access. Its upper branches appear full of life with 12 species of epiphite living and blooming on its trunk including

Azaleas, Rhododendrons and Mountain ash.

KIGEN SUGI （紀元杉）

Height: 19.5m

Trunk circumference: 8.1m

Age: 3000 years old

Access: On the mountain road to Yodogawa Trail Entrance (above Yakusugiland)

This is one of the most accessible ancient Yakusugi trees as it is quite literally beside the road. It is not only one tree but the host of a variety of other species of trees and plants that live on its weathered body. These include Hinoki cypress, Yamaguruma and Hikagetsutsuji. It also displays the blossoms of Yakushima Rhododendron in early summer.

THE FAUNA

Since Yakushima separated from the Kyushu mainland some 15,000 years ago, the environment of the island has produced a rich and quasi-primitive habitat.

There are various subspecies that are endemic to Yakushima, the most well-known of which the Yaku-macaques and the Yaku dear. There are also 150 bird species, 15

species of reptiles, 8 species of amphibians, and approximately 1,900 species of insects which have been confirmed to inhabit Yakushima, making this small island extremely abundant in fauna.

YAKU MACAQUES

（ヤクザル） *Macaca fuscata yakui*

This subspecies of the Japanese Macaque can only be found in the wild on Yakushima Island. They are fairly short and stout compared to their mainland cousins, at an average height of 50 cm and weight of 10 kg, and their fur is longer and thicker.

Estimates on their numbers lie at around 6,000 and as they roam freely on the mountains mostly in small groups of four to five, can often be seen in the forest, near the main road and sometimes in the villages.

The macaques have the freedom of the island but are frequently found in the laurel forests where there are berry-bearing trees. They spend their days foraging, grooming and carefully picking bugs from each other's fur. Their diet consists mainly of berries from bayberry （ヤマモモ） and Japanese fig （イヌビワ） plants in early summer and acorns （ドングリ） in autumn/winter. They are, however, far from fussy and eat over a hundred different types of plants as well as mushrooms （キノコ） and insects.

If you come across a troop, they usually scamper away. But sometimes if you keep your head down and avoid eye contact, they

will ignore you and allow you to observe them. The babies (born in the spring after the snow has thawed) are especially curious. They are invariably with their mothers, often riding on their backs for up to a year.

There are many places you may come across monkeys. They can often be seen loitering at the roadside on the road to Yakusugiland, particularly early morning and late afternoon. They are of course waiting for passing tourists to throw them food, who despite the signs saying otherwise, get so excited at seeing them that they throw all kinds of junk out of the window with amazing consistency. This familiarity with human food sources has led to all kinds of problems with local people.

For many of the farmers on the island, the monkeys are little more than pests who destroy their crops on a regular basis. Ponkan and Tonkan citrus fruit, both of which resemble small oranges, are a favourite of the macaques and there has been a battle raging between them and the farmers for many years. In 1989, as much as ¥10 million was recorded in damage from macaques in the north part of the island. It is now common to see electric fences surrounding the citrus groves to prevent damage but this kind of protection is expensive and a large number of monkeys are captured and killed, either by professional hunters or in crude farmers' traps.

YAKUSHIKA DEER

(ヤクシカ) *Cervus nippon yakushimae*

The Yakushika are another subspecies of the mainland deer. They number around 7,000 and are a common sight in the mountains. Like the macaques they are smaller than the mainland species. They can often be seen following troops of macaques and scavenging on the fruit they drop from the trees.

They used to hold a spiritual place in the beliefs of islanders who traditionally held them to be the messengers of 'Ippon Hoju Daigongen', the God of the mountain. That belief is no longer widely held and although officially protected, there is now an annual hunting season and, like the macaques, farmers trap them as pests on their land. It is not just the locals however who have problems with the deer.

Environmentalists wishing to protect the rare plants and trees on Yakushima have found that their efforts at conservation have mostly been eaten by ever increasing numbers of deer. Research is being carried out at present as to the extent of this destruction by fencing off key areas of forest and comparing these with the growth of the unfenced areas around them and some kind of balance is sought between the continued presence of deer and the flora of the forest.

OTHER MAMMALS

Other mammals, none of which you are likely to see on a short visit, include the Siberian weasel, Japanese mole, Small/ Large Japanese field mouse, horse shoe bat and the unfortunate recent introduction of raccoon dogs to Yakushima's fragile natural habitat.

INSECTS

If you walk through the forests of Yakushima, you cannot fail but notice that it is alive with insects of all shapes and sizes. Despite their often strange appearance most are perfectly harmless, but of the 19,000 species of insects living on Yakushima, there are a handful that needs to be treated with caution.

MUKADE (百足) are large reddish brown centipedes with yellow-orange legs. They could be anywhere between 10 - 20 cm long and can move very fast when disturbed. A bite from a mukade can cause serious swelling and considerable pain, and if bitten, it is advisable to seek medical attention. Locals kill mukade on sight. Folklore suggests burning it or it will return from the dead to take revenge but a simple squash would suffice. Be watchful for them after heavy rain and especially around rainy season when they seek shelter inside.

SUZUMEBACHI HORNETS (大雀蜂) are the world's largest hornets and can be very aggressive if they detect a threat to their hive or food sources. They have a rather nasty sting much more toxic than a standard bee or wasp. General advice to prevent the unlikely interest of hornets in the mountains is to avoid strong perfumes, avoid wearing black and keep to the mountain paths. It is a common belief among farmers that the strength of the following typhoon season can be judged by the height of the hornets' nests in the trees. Low nests mean the storms will be severe and high that they will be mild.

JAPANESE GROUND BEETLES (マイマイカブリ) are common small black beetles with a long snout they use to eat snails with. When threatened they spray an acid mixture into the air which if it reaches your eyes will be very painful. Handle these with caution.

SNAKES

There are a variety of common snakes on Yakushima like the **Japanese rat snake** and the **Oriental Odd-tooth** but there are two that anyone venturing into the forest need to know about:

• **MAMUSHI** (ニホンマムシ) or **PIT VIPER** has a dark colour and,

like most vipers, has a distinctive triangular shaped head. Their bite is poisonous and very serious especially in the very young and old. Incidences of attacks are rare but they do happen: An elderly neighbour was killed by a mamushi while tending his field in Anbo and Kashima-san (of Kashima Kougei Crafts) was temporarily paralysed in one side of his body after being bitten on the finger.

• **YAMAKAGASHI** (ヤマカガシ) or **TIGER KEELBACK** has an irregular brown pattern with some reddish smudges and black stripes. These are often lurking around streams and rivers and as long as you walk slowly and firmly you have little chance of catching it basking in the sun within biting distance. It is poisonous however and its bite can be very serious. Its fangs are located at the back of its mouth which thankfully makes biting a large object like you and me a much more difficult prospect.

BIRDS

More than 150 bird species live on Yakushima. This includes endemic species like the **Yakushima varied tit**, distinctively smaller than the mainland tit, and the **Yakushima Narcissus Flycatcher**, lighter in colour than its mainland equivalent and with a distinctive yellow chest. There are other threatened species such as the **Japanese wood pigeon**, **Izu Leaf-warbler**, and the **Izu thrush** which is easy to spot with its distinctive colouring - dark plumage, yellow eye rings and bill, brown wings, and a red chest. The **Ryukyu robin** is considered so important that it has even been declared a Japanese Natural Monument.

SEA CREATURES

The **Kuroshio Current** (黒潮) splits south of Yakushima and flows both sides of the island, wrapping it in all year round warm seas. The average sea temperature is between 20 to 30°c and to illustrate how warm this is, as a fisherman on a flying fish trawler in chilly weather, I used to throw a bucket over the side and warm my cold hands in the water. This warmth allows a huge variety of fish to inhabit the waters around the island - there are thought to be at least 580 different species of fish.

There are also over 100 different species of coral that surround the island. They are a mixture of both temperate and tropical but, like much of the coral worldwide, are under threat due to 'coral bleaching'. This is the absence of an essential plant plankton called Kacchuso (*zooxanthella*) causing the coral to whiten and die.

Of the many creatures inhabiting the sea around Yakushima, there are two species which are synonymous with the island:

LOGGERHEAD TURTLES (アカ ウミガメ) & GREEN TURTLES (ア オウミガメ)

Both Loggerhead and Green Turtles are frequent visitors to Yakushima from May to July and many of them were born on the island's beaches. There are several official turtle nesting sites on the western side of the island where most of the turtles arrive but any one of the beaches around the coast can receive the turtles.

Loggerhead turtle

In the Nagata area there are three sandy beaches in a row. Maehama, in front of Nagata village, Inakahama, the longest stretch of sandy beach on the island (800 m), and Yotsusehama further north. The astonishing fact is that between them, these three beaches make up 40% of all loggerhead nesting in Japan. And because of this they are now protected as a 'Wetland of International Importance' under the Ramsar Convention.

Every year about 500 loggerhead turtles lay their eggs here. Female turtles start arriving between May and July to crawl up the beach, dig a hole with their back flippers and deposit 80-130 perfectly rounded eggs. Then 45-70 days later the eggs hatch and baby turtles scuttle down the beach to the sea. It is believed, though, that only 1 in 5,000 of these baby turtles actually reach maturity and will return one day to the island.

FLYING FISH (飛び魚)

In May 2008, an NHK Japanese television crew filmed a flying fish off the coast of Yakushima which instantly made world news. It flew for 45 seconds and is thought to be one of the longest recorded flights by any flying fish (the previous record being 42 seconds in the 1920s).

Flying fish (known as 'Tobiuo' in Japanese) are able to fly because they have developed enlarged pectoral fins. They swim towards the surface of the water at great speed, leap through at a shallow angle and then, like an aeroplane, accelerate to take-off speed with their lateral fins spread wide and their tails beating the water. They then glide until there is no more lift and slide back into the water like Olympic divers.

It is thought that flying fish fly mainly to escape from predators, particularly dolphin fish or shira (シイラ) and it is very common for dolphin fish to be caught in fishing nets alongside them. When dolphin fish are caught they regurgitate the contents of their stomachs and these are usually the rotting carcasses of flying fish.

POPULATION

People have been living on Yakushima since around 2000-1000 BC when it was known as the barbarous Yaku region. Its inhabitants were the **Jomon people** (縄文人) known for their distinctive rope-patterned pottery. In more recent times, the name Yakushima crops up here and there in Japanese history linked to random events like the visiting of a Chinese envoy in the 8th century and the landing of an Italian missionary named *Sidocchi* in the 18th century, both of which suggest a sizable population. The current population is around 14,000 but as in the region of 315,000 tourists visit every year, it often feels much greater.

YAKUSHIMA FOLKLORE

The following are a collection of local stories and legends involving creatures that were believed to influence life on Yakushima. They form part of the distinctive culture of Yakushima and were relayed to me by local people many of whom firmly believed in what they were telling. The grandfather of one of my neighbours, for example, swore that he had seen a Garappa in the local river and gave detailed descriptions about what it looked like and how it moved. Younger generations are not quite so convinced but they still know the stories all the same.

1. YAMA-NO-ONSUKE

One autumn, a hunter named Sasaki went to set a monkey trap with his brother between Nanako dake and Eboshi dake near **Yudomari.** It was getting dark so they decided to stay in Arake-no-miso, a shelter in the rocks.

After dinner, his brother went to sleep, but he stayed up and enjoyed the warmth of the fire. Out of the forest he suddenly heard a shout 'O-i' so he left the fire and looked around to see who was there. No one was there but then he heard it again so he decided to reply with the same shrill 'O-i'. Nothing happened. But his shout had woken his brother who immediately told him to stop. Refusing to divulge why, he forbade him to answer any call in the mountains. Sasaki was curious so he repeatedly asked his brother why until his brother eventually whispered in the quietest voice he could, that it was 'Yama-no-Onsuke'.

After a while the voice came again but it sounded much louder and clearer. Sasaki was so surprised to hear it at such a close distance that he replied instinctively. He regretted this immediately when the voice then screamed behind him. Silence followed so he picked up a stick and waited. The sound came again even closer. He threw a piece of burning firewood to where he thought the voice was but could see nothing.

What followed was a sleepless night of scraping noises coming from the rock above their heads, the sounds of trees falling and rocks tumbling. As much as they wanted to return, they had to stay another night to tend the monkey trap but that night was even worse. Even shooting their gun in the air did not stop the noise.

2. THE GODS OF MOCHOMU MOUNTAIN

One day an old man from Onoaida took his grandson to Miyakata, a mountain at the foot of **Mochomu dake**, to pick firewood. While the old man and the boy were searching the undergrowth for sticks and fallen branches, a warm wind began to blow and the grass swayed strongly back and forth. The sound of a flute then followed and they could see the light of lanterns at the forest edge.

The old man had experienced this before and knew it to be a sign that the gods were passing. In October every year (October was known as 'no god month' [神無月] in the old Japanese calender) all the gods in Yakushima went from Mochomu to a mountain called Wariishi dake. Fearing for the safety of his grandson, he instructed him to quickly lower his head while they passed.

But the grandson was curious like all little boys his age and he raised his head just in time to see something moving smoothly above the grass. He just had time to see a creature with a red face, a white beard and white clothes disappearing towards Mochomu Mountain, before suddenly became profoundly and permanently deaf.

3. THE VANISHING DEER ANTLERS

One clear autumn evening a local man named Sasaki, who was staying at the mountain shelter of Detaro iwaya, wandered off to hunt deer. He sat down on a yakusugi stump and blew three times on his deer whistle to attract deer. He waited for a return call to signal a deer coming into his trap but instead he heard whispering. He jumped up and searched around but no one appeared to be there. He returned to the stump, blew the whistle again but the same thing happened. He moved closer to the sound and as he did he saw a round black object twice the size of a human head.

Little creatures were coming out of the black ball and when he looked closer, they turned out to be long-legged frogs. He picked up a branch, hit the black object and hundreds of frogs dispersed in all directions. Underneath where the frogs had been he noticed an antler. He picked it up but it was slimy so he washed it in a nearby stream. It immediately became brittle and snapped.

He then clearly understood why he had seen so few fallen antlers on his mountain trips - frogs eat the antlers – dissolving it with their mucous. He relayed this story to his disbelieving friends back in the village but to no avail until a year later his friend saw the same spectacle and knowledge of the frogs in **Hana-no-ego** became widespread.

4. YAMAHIME (山姫)

One fine day, a farmer named Nagoe, went to *Jigokudani* behind **Miyanoura dake** to cut and collect bamboo trees. When he cut into the first bamboo, it began to pour with rain so he stopped, wiped the water off his face and tightened the straw shawl that kept the rain off. He heard a noise in the forest ahead and looked up. There, just inside the clearing, stood a beautiful woman in a bright, clean kimono. Before he could call out he was dazzled by a blinding light and was pushed backwards so forcibly that he landed flat on his back. It rained harder and harder and slowly he looked up from the ground. The woman was coming towards him.

He panicked, flung himself prostrate on the forest floor and begged for forgiveness promising he would never come here again. When he looked up again, she had stopped and was smiling at him. He prostrated himself again and recited prayers until he was so hoarse he could speak no more. Eventually the rain stopped. And when he gathered the courage to look up again she was gone. So he left all of the bamboo where it was and ran straight home, where he promptly fell ill and was bed ridden for a week.

This was Yamahime, the beautiful mountain princess. Legend says that when seen, she is so utterly beautiful that it is impossible to leave her gaze. Her hair is flowing and glistening, her skin pale as the moonlight and she is dressed in an immaculate red kimono. She smiles at her victims and if the smile is returned, she steals their life in an instant.

5. GARAPPA (ガラッパ)

An old man once went to **Anbo River** to wash his horse but the horse refused to get into the water. Annoyed at this, he tugged the horse by its reigns and forced it to bathe in the cool waters. Once the horse was clean the man returned home but he was quickly overcome by illness and was bed-ridden. He was told that this was the result of a curse by a Garappa.

A few days before a forest worker from Kosugidani, a village high in the mountains, had committed suicide and the rain had washed his dead body down to the river mouth. The Garappa, the water gods of Yakushima, had been holding a meeting about what to do with the corpse, when the man had disturbed and angered them. On hearing this, the old man returned to the same place at the riverside and apologised to where he thought the Garappa might be. His apology worked and he promptly recovered.

6. TENGU (天狗)

In October every year all the gods of Yakushima go to Izumo in Shimane Prefecture in the Chugoku region of mainland Japan. Without the gods to keep order in the mountains, all manner of lesser creatures descend out of the forest to celebrate. One of these is the Tengu, supernatural creatures with obscenely long noses or beaks, and they can be heard beating their drums on the mountain side throughout October. They gradually increase in volume during the night with the rhythm much faster towards sunrise until quiet descends on the forest at daybreak.

When walking in the mountains it is a common sight to see pine trees with branches crowded unnaturally together. This is because the first day of every month Tengu descend

to the coast to retrieve water and on the way they rest on the branches. It is commonly known that anyone who cuts down these pine trees will be cursed forever by a Tengu. People are therefore reluctant to even go near these trees. If however one must be cut down, the night before an axe is put beside it and left until morning. If it is still in place the following day, the tree can be cut down. If the axe has fallen to the ground, the tree cannot be touched for fear of bringing the wrath of the Tengu.

CLIMATE

The climate of Yakushima varies very much depending on altitude. Around the coast it is considered to be sub-tropical, although it gets distinctly chilly in winter. As you rise up the Mae dake (the frontal range) mountains around the coast it changes to warm temperate and then as you reach the central band of mountains in the centre of the island, it changes to cool-temperate. From here upwards to the summits, it is sub-Alpine.

	Av Temp	Max Temp	Min Temp
Jan	12.3	15.3	9
Feb	14.4	17.1	11.5
March	14.5	17.5	11.6
April	20.2	23.7	17.1
May	22.8	25.6	20.2
June	24.3	27.3	21.6
July	27	30.8	23.6
Aug	28	32.2	24.2
Sept	26.4	29.6	23.6
Oct	23.3	26	20.6
Nov	18.7	21.6	15.6
Dec	15	17.7	12.2

Temperatures (°C) in Yakushima

So while the weather is usually mild around the coast, the inner mountains have a climate much more resembling Hokkaido in northern Japan. The average temperatures lie somewhere around 20 °c around the coast and 15 °c inland around Kosugidani, although the heat can be almost unbearable in summer and thick snow falls on the high mountains every winter as it reaches well below zero.

There are however variations on the above depending on how high you are on the mountains.

The general rule is that for every 100 m you climb the temperature decreases by 0.6° c. This means that you should allow for the following temperature changes in the mountains:

• At **Shiratani Unsuikyo** (825 m) it is 5°c below.

• At **Jomon Sugi** (1300m) the temperature is 7.8 °c below the temperatures in the above table.

• At **Takatsu hut** (1330 m) it is 8°c below.

• At **Yodogawa hut** (1380 m) it is 8.3°c below.

• At **Shintakatsu hut** (1460 m) it is 8.8 °c below.

• At **Shikanosawa hut** (1550 m) it is 9.3°c below.

• At **Ishizuka hut** (1600 m) it is 9.6 °c below.

• At the summit of **Mt.Miyanoura** (1936 m) it is 11.6°c below.

Most people have heard about the legendary rainfall. The often quoted 35 days a month rain was actually taken from a popular novel published in the 1950s named 'Floating cloud' or '**Ukigumo**' (浮雲) by **Fumiko Hayashi** (林芙美子), who once lived in Anbo in Yakushima and in which key scenes take place in the book.

The apparently high annual rainfall figure of 4,000 mm on the coast is deceptive. It does indeed rain but not as much as you might think with the 35 days claims. Half an hour of rain, a ray of sun, low clouds, a spot of rain again, cloud, and then boom, clear skies out of nowhere. The average visitor is usually far more confused about the weather than wet and soggy. Having said that though, when in the high mountains, there is much less confusion.

The average rainfall reaches up to 10,000 mm per year up here and the summits are often covered in dense cloud or mist. Unless the sky is clear of cloud expect the worst. There are two very notable additions to the general climate of Yakushima: Rainy season and typhoon season. Both have the ability to change travel plans in an instant.

RAINY SEASON (June/July) appears suddenly in early summer and levels of over 80% humidity can make hiding from the rain indoors quite uncomfortable and sticky. The general pattern is that it rains very hard most of the day but by early evening the skies clear and you ponder about all the things you could have done if the day had been like that from the start.

TYPHOON SEASON (Sept/ Oct)

can shut down the island for several days depending on the location and size of the storm. Well before the storm arrives the waves change shape and height and there is a distinctive feel to a pre-typhoon wave which is highly effective at inducing nausea.

When the typhoon gets closer the transport links shut down one by one. The fishing boats cannot leave port with wave heights over three metres and the jet foils usually stop operations any higher. The ferry can last a little longer but that too stops as the waves increase. The last to leave is the plane which gets busy with all the extra passengers from the boats. If you missed that, you would have to wait it out and join the rest of the island in boarding up, tying everything down and listening for bulletins over the loud speakers.

Typhoons invariably change direction and head on to terrorize China or into the Pacific. Occasionally however they hit full on with explosive force.

TYPHOON 17

Several years on and there has yet to be anything quite like Typhoon Nabi (No.17 in the Japanese system). This was a category 5 super typhoon that formed on Aug 29th 2005 east of Saipan. It was of a similar strength to Hurricane Katrina which at the same time was devastating the southern States of the USA. It hit Yakushima in the early hours of Sept 6th and went on the following day to damage 10,000 homes, cause 168 landslides, and led to 143 injuries and 21 deaths on mainland Japan. Typhoon No.17 was travelling at a speed of 15 kph and because of this its full force lingered for two whole days.

Typhoon 17

As was customary in any typhoon, the power station in the mountains above Anbo was hit by lightening and the electricity supply was cut by mid-evening.

By candle-light we cowered under a makeshift shelter of futons and pillows as the winds reached 160 kph and the waves a massive 9 m.

Our rented home was a sprawling wooden country house which was on the verge of being swallowed by the forest. In fact for forest creatures our house was merely an extension, with praying mantis, wolf spiders, centipedes and untold crawling things as permanent residents.

The wind pounded the north side of the house the whole day of the

Sept 5th which was not so bad as it had the least windows. Logic dictated that we spent the night at the other end of the house. The only real option in this part of our old crumbly house was the annex room that jutted out into the garden.

At first this was fine but in the early hours, the wind and the noise suddenly dropped. It was like flipping the off-switch. Insects were chirping, there were stars in the sky. Once the eye of the storm had passed over however, it all kicked off again but the direction of the gusts had changed. A wind of stunning ferocity was slamming into the sliding glass panels that lined three sides of the room.

We all feared the worse, dived under our bedding and hoped to last the night. In the end we did and by sunrise the house was still intact (-ish) and the winds calming. We ventured out to count our losses shortly after (one car, one roof and one cat) and ponder the raw power of nature.

2: GETTING THERE & BACK

BY AIR

Japan Air Commuter (日本エアコミューター), a division of JAL, operates daily flights from the following places:

1 VIA KAGOSHIMA (鹿児島)

KAGOSHIMA → YAKUSHIMA

08.30	09.05
10.40	11.15
14.30	15.10
15.50	16.30
16.45	17.20

YAKUSHIMA → KAGOSHIMA

09.30	10.05
12.20	12.55
14.15	14.50
16.55	17.30
17.45	18.20

Price varies according to the season and how far in advance you book. As a rough guide, one way should be around ¥13,000 and return ¥26,000.

2 VIA FUKUOKA (福岡)

FUKUOKA → YAKUSHIMA

12.30	13.40

YAKUSHIMA → FUKUOKA

15.35	16.45

Price varies according to the season and how far in advance you book. As a rough guide, one way should be around ¥25,000 and return ¥45,000.

3 VIA OSAKA (大阪)

YAKUSHIMA → OSAKA

11.40	13.05

OSAKA → YAKUSHIMA

10.25	11.55

Price varies according to the season and how far in advance you book. As a rough guide, one way should be around ¥34,000 and return ¥62,000.

Timetables are prone to change so check with JAL for current timetables before making plans. 🖥 jal.co.jp

BY SEA

Kagoshima Port (鹿児島港)

If you come via Kagoshima airport and catch a ferry or jet foil please note that the airport is over 50 min by road north of the port.

There is a shuttle bus, called the **Airport limousine bus** (空港リムジンバス), which for ¥1,200 takes you to Kagoshima Main port (鹿児島 本港). The bus for Kagoshima city is line No.2 and colour coded in red. Note that not all buses go as far as the port. Only bus times in bold go on to the port terminal (高速船ターミナル), the others stop in the city centre.

Kagoshima Bus timetable

8	30 40
9	**00** 10 20 **40**
10	**00** 20 **40**
11	**00 20 40**
12	**00** 20 30 40
13	**00 20 40**
14	**00 20** 30 **40**
15	00 **20 40**
16	00 20 40
17	00 **20 40**
18	00 20 **40**
19	**00** 20 45
20	55
21	**05**

If you arrive at **Kagoshima Chuo Train Station** (鹿児島中央駅) a taxi takes 15 min, the Rosen bus (路線バス) takes 20 min and the 'Dolphin 150' shuttle bus (ドルフィン 150) takes 16 min (both from stand 5)to the Dolphin port which is only a short walk to the South Wharf terminals.

Airport limousine bus

Facing Sakurajima, the Tane-Yaku jetfoil terminal is the triangular building to the left. Go further into the port area and the Mishima and Toshima terminals are on the left and right respectively. The South

Wharf passenger terminal is at the end and Ferry Yakushima 2 leaves to the right of this.

BY JET FOIL

TANE-YAKU JET FOIL (ジェットフォイル「トッピー」「ロケット」)

Price can depend on the season but it should be around ¥7,700 one way and ¥14,000 return. Up-to-date information can be found at 🖥 tykousoku.jp (in Japanese).

KAGOSHIMA → YAKUSHIMA

07.30 T	10.10 M
07.45 I	09.45 M
09.10 T	11.45 M
10.30 T	13.20 A
12.00	13.45 M
13.20	15.10 M
16.00 T	18.30 A

YAKUSHIMA → KAGOSHIMA

07.00 A, T	09.35
10.00 M, T	12.40
10.45 M	12.30
12.00 M	13.45
13.30 A	15.30
15.00 M, T	17.40
16.20 M, T, I	19.15

M= To/from Miyanoura (宮之浦)

A = To/from Anbo (安房)

T = Stops at Nishinoomote (西之表) in Tanegashima (種子島)

I = Stops at Ibusuki (指宿)

If there is bad weather and the wave height rises above 3 m both jet foils may be cancelled. You can get a refund if you have bought your ticket already. If they are cancelled, try the ferry as it often continues to run or try the plane which rarely cancels due to the weather.

Tane-Yaku jet foil

NOTE: If you want to reserve a boat and you do not speak Japanese, your accommodation may help. Shikinoyado Onoaida and Morinokokage, for example, provide this service for their guests (see the accommodation section).

BY FERRY

1. FERRY YAKUSHIMA 2
(フェリー屋久島 2)

KAGOSHIMA→ YAKUSHIMA

08.30	12.30

YAKUSHIMA→ KAGOSHIMA

13.30	17.40

The ferry is large and comfortable and provides a carpeted area to lie down on. If you have the time, it is a scenic way to arrive as you can appreciate the size and shape of the island as it draws closer.

It operates from Kagoshima South Port to Miyanoua port (宮之浦港) in Yakushima. The price varies according to season but should be

around ¥4,600 one way and ¥7,900 return. Up to date prices and timetables can be found at 🖥 f2.dion.ne.jp/~orita.k

2. FERRY HIBISCUS
(フェリーはいびすかす)

KAGOSHIMA → YAKUSHIMA

18.00 → 21.40 → 05.10 → 07.00

YAKUSHIMA → KAGOSHIMA

08.20 → 10.10 → 11.00 → 14.40

This ferry operates from a different port in Kagoshima called **Taniyama Port** (谷山港). It takes about 15 minutes by taxi (¥1,100) or 40 minutes by bus from Yamagataya bus terminal (at Tenmonkan) in the city center. There is only 1 bus a day at 16.20 (¥370). The return bus is at 15.14 (¥400) and it leaves across the main road to the port.

The fare should be around ¥3,200 one way and ¥6,400 return. But be warned this ferry is cheap for a reason, you have to sleep in a shared carpeted area while it docks for the night in Tanegashima. You are not permitted to go ashore until you reach Yakushima the following day. Returning from Yakushima is more convenient but very slow.

Ferry Yakushima 2

3 MOVING AROUND

SUZUKI RENTALEASE
Miyanoura 2395-32
Tel: 0997-42-1772 Fax: 0997-42-0307
We rent cars and 50cc bikes with
written explanations in English
http://www4.synapse.ne.jp/rentacar/
Email: nakashima@po3.synapse.ne.jp

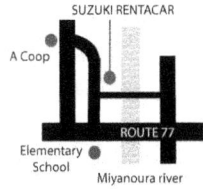

**We welcome
non-Japanese
visitors!**

SUZUKI RENTACAR
A Coop
ROUTE 77
Elementary
School
Miyanoura river

The best way of moving around Yakushima depends on many variables: the duration of your stay, the time of year, your destinations, your inclinations etc. Most people tend to hire a car but the day 'free pass' may make the bus a more viable option. Scooters and motorbikes can be rented, or mountain bikes if you do not mind the ups and downs. Walking is of course the mode of transport of the mountains and it is quite feasible to walk from the port in Miyanoura straight to the Shiratani mountain hut and across the island without the need of anything save for two, soon to be very weary, legs.

BY CAR

The most convenient way to travel in Yakushima is by rental car and there are many car hire outlets on the island competing with each other. Most of the companies are near the airport in Koseda and the ports in Miyanoura and Anbo. The local companies tend to be cheaper than the national ones but it is worth shopping around for the best deal at the time you want to visit. Also **check with your accommodation** as they sometimes have car hire services.

If you do not speak Japanese, some car hire websites in English like **ToCoo!** (www2.tocoo.jp) cover Yakushima. SuzukiRentalease have English documentation (see below) and also some English speaking accommodation options will help you hire a car. Look for the ☺ sign in the accommodation section and contact them.

Miyanoura area

• ☺ **Suzuki Rentalease** (70 cars) (スズキレンタリース屋久島) ☎ 42-1772 🖥 www4.synapse.ne.jp/rentacar

• **Mazda Rentacar** (19 cars) (マツダレンタカー) Miyanoura: ☎ 42-2401 🖥 mazda-rentacar.co.jp (☺ English website)

• **Matsubanda Rentacar** (58 cars) (まつばんだレンタカー) ☎ 43-5000 🖥 yakushima.co.jp

• **Nansei Rentacar** (15 cars) (南星レンタカー) ☎ 42-2115 🖥 nansei-car.com

• **Kumage Rentacar** (19 cars) (熊毛レンタカー) ☎ 42-2756 🖥 www5.ocn.ne.jp/~kumaren

• **Toyota Rentalease** (トヨタ レンタリース鹿児島) (96 cars) ☎ 42-2000 🖥 rent.toyota.co.jp/top.asp

• **Orix Rentacar** (25 cars) (オリック スレンタカー) ☎ 42-2669 💻 car.orix.co.jp/rent/shop

• **Yakushima Kankosha** (21 cars) (屋久島観光社) ☎ 42-0036

Airport area

• **Nippon Rentacar** (20 cars) (ニッ ポンレンタカー) ☎ 49-4189 💻 nipponrentacar.co.jp (☺ English website)

• **Mazda Rentacar** (19 cars) (マツダ レンタカー) ☎ 43-5700 💻 mazda-rentacar.co.jp (☺ English website)

• **Airport Rentacar NAVI** (24 cars) (空港レンタカーNAVI) ☎ 43-5068

• **Michi-no-eki** (屋久島道の駅観光) (20 cars) ☎ 49-1216 ☎ 0992014110 💻 ymktour.net/car. Also has camping cars (キャンピング カー)

• **Toyota Rentalease** (トヨタ レンタ リース鹿児島) (96 cars)☎ 43-5180 💻 rent.toyota.co.jp/top.asp

• **Orix Rentacar** (25 cars) (オリック スレンタカー) ☎ 43-5888 💻 car.orix.co.jp/rent/shop

Anbo area

• **San Paulo Rentacar** (サンパウロレ ンタカー) ☎ 46-3848 💻 www12.ocn.ne.jp/~sanpauro ✉ sanpauro@mocha.ocn.ne.jp

• **Kamiyama Rentacar** (21 cars) (カ ミヤマレンタカー) ☎ 49-7070 💻 www2.ocn.ne.jp/~ky-kanko

• **Anbo Shinjiyama Rentacar** (安房 しんじやまレンタカー) (16 cars) ☎ 49-7277 💻 ww9.ocn.ne.jp/~anboh

Onoaida area

• **Niizato Rentacar** (にいざとレンタカ ー) ☎ 47-2511 (4 cars) 💻 nizato2511.web.fc2.com

Hirauchi area

• **Yakushima Youth Hostel** (屋久島 ユースホステル) ☎ 47-3751 💻 yakushima-yh.net

The prices range between ¥4,000-¥6,000 for 1 day and ¥8,000-¥10,000 for 2 days for the smallest car; then for a medium car (1500cc), 1 day is ¥6,000 to ¥8,000 and 2 days ¥12,000 and ¥15,000; a more powerful car (2000cc) rises to ¥13,000 for 1 day and ¥22,000 for 2 days; and should you require a people wagon for 6-7 people, 1 day's rental is around ¥13,000 to ¥16,000. The minimum rental period is 6 hours and then it rises to 9, 12, 24, 36 and 48 hours. If you require a car for longer than 48 hours, it must be by the day not the hour. So the minimum after 48 hours is 72 hours. Should you then be late in returning the car, any extra time is by the hour.

The one essential thing you need if you do not have a Japanese licence is an **international driving licence**. Without this you will not be allowed to rent.

The roads, bar one or two mountain tracks, are sealed and well maintained and driving on Yakushima is relatively uncomplicated. There is essentially one continuous road around the island with only a handful of traffic signals in the larger villages and anyone used to driving on the mainland will be pleasantly surprised. Some of the car parks are virtually non-existent, as at Oko-no-taki for example, so be prepared to park in tight spots by the road side (watch out for unprotected drains running at the side of the road).

Be aware that police speed traps operate frequently on Yakushima's roads and eager policemen with speed guns have a habit of hiding behind bushes on bends in the road before or after a village. So be warned and keep to the speed limits.

Also watch out for deer who like to roam around the roads at night playing chicken with speeding cars. So again drive with caution and keep to the speed limits.

BY BUS

There are two main bus companies that run routes on Yakushima: the Yakushima Koutsu Bus (屋久島交通バス) and the Matsubanda bus (まつばんだ交通バス).

The **Yakushima Koutsu Bus** has a one or two day bus pass. It's called a **Free pass** (フリー乗車券). 1 day costs ¥2,000 for an adult and ¥1,000 for children and a 2 day pass costs ¥3,000 and ¥1,500 respectively. You can get on and off the bus as many times as you want but it is only valid for the Yakushima Koutsu bus *NOT* the Matsubanda bus.

You cannot buy the pass on the bus – but you can buy it at these places:

Miyanoura area

- **Miyanoura port** (宮之浦港)

- **Yakushima Kanko Centre** (屋久島観光センター)

- ☺ **Port side Youth Hostel** (ポートサイドユースホステル)

Koseda area

- **Yakushima airport counter** (屋久島空港カウンター)

Anbo area

- **Anbo Port** (安房港)

- **Mori-no-kirameki** (森のきらめき) at the junction near the police station.

- **Yakusugi Museum** (屋久杉自然館)

Onoaida area

- ☺ **JR Hotel** (ＪＲホテル屋久島)

Hirauchi area

- ☺ **Yakushima Youth Hostel** (屋久島ユースホステル)

See the back of the book for details of bus timetables.

BY SCOOTER

Motorbikes or scooters can be rented at these places:

Miyanoura area

- ☺ **Suzuki Rentalease** (スズキレンタリース) offers 50cc bikes for rent. ☎ 42-1772 🖥 www4.synapse.ne.jp /rentacar (See ad for more details)

Anbo area

- **You Shop Nangoku** (南国) also offers 50cc bikes. ☎ 46-2705 🖥 ww14.ocn.ne.jp/~nangoku/sub1.html

Hirauchi area

• **Yakushima Youth Hostel** (屋久島 ユースホステル) has 50cc bikes for rent. ☎ 47-3751 💻 yakushima-yh.net

The price for the first day ranges from ¥3,500 to ¥4,000 and then ¥3,000 every day after that. If 2 people ride together on the same bike, it is an extra ¥500.

BY BICYCLE

Bicycles are fairly cheap and easy to rent and are a great way to experience the best of the island. There are plenty of ups and downs on the coastal road and as long as you prepare yourself that it will not all be hands-free gliding, it is a very enjoyable and rewarding activity. The only really taxing parts of the coastal road are the ascents on the Seibu Rindo in the West of the island. Should you wish to circumnavigate the island in one go, it takes around 8-9 hours and is probably easier travelling clockwise.

Bike rental requires a deposit for the time you have rented the bike and costs usually around ¥1,200 a day for a mountain bike. **Check with your accommodation** or try the following:

• **Suzuki Rentalease** (スズキレンタ リース) 💻 (See ad for more details) www4.synapse.ne.jp/rentacar

• **Furusatoichiba** (ふるさと市場) 💻 yakushima.co.jp/ichiba

• **Yakushima Youth Hostel** 💻 yakushima-yh.net

Midori no kaze rentacycle (緑の風 レンタサイクル)

💻 xn-3iqs55ayoa25z.com/shop/midorinokaze (Yes, this really is their email address) is a scheme whereby you can rent from one place and drop off at another. The cost of renting a bike through this scheme is only ¥800 a day for a mountain bike (¥500 for a 3-gear bike) but bikes need to be reserved through Yakushima Kanko centre. The following are part of the scheme:

Miyanoura area

• **Yakushima Kanko Centre** (屋久島 観光センター) 💻 yksm.com 🕐 08.00-19.00 ☎ 42-0091

• **Minshuku Manten** (民宿まんてん) ☎ 42-1180

• **Miyanourasou** (宮之浦荘) ☎ 42-1352

• **Uchida Sekiyu gas station** (内田石 油) 🕐 08.00-18.00 Closed New Year ☎ 42-0722

Koseda area

• **Nanho Sekiyu gas station** (南邦石 油) 🕐 08.00-19.00 ☎ 43-5321

Anbo area

• **Mori-no-kirameki** (森のきらめき) 🕐 07.30-19.00 ☎ 49-7101 (See accommodation section)

• **Daichan House** (大ちゃんハウス) ☎ 46-3565 (See accommodation section)

• **Minshuku Suginosato** (民宿杉の 里) ☎ 46-2919

Mugio area

- **Botanical Research Park** (ボタニカルリサーチパーク) ⏰ 08.30-17.00 ☎ 47-2636

Hara area

- **Minshuku Sansui** (民宿山水) ☎ 47-3411

Onoaida area

- **Hidaka Sekiyu gas station** (日高石油) ⏰ 07.00-18.30 ☎ 47-2946

Hirauchi area

- **Kaichu onsen sou** (海中温泉荘) ☎ 47-2403

- **Kaisenchaya Bungalow** (海鮮茶屋 バンガロー) ☎ 47-3322

Kurio area

- **S Mart** (Sマート) ⏰ 06.30-18.00 ☎ 48-2805

Nagata area

- **Maruso Sekiyu gas station** (まるそう石油) ⏰ 07.30-18.00. Closed New Year ☎ 45-2103

Isso area

- **Higo Sekiyu gas station** (肥後 石油) ⏰ 07.00-19.00. Closed Sun ☎ 44-2102

BY TAXI

Taxis are often invaluable when arriving and departing but hikers also often use taxis to take and collect them from the mountain trails in the early hours of the morning and late afternoon. Should you need one, get the help of your accommodation, go to the taxi offices or phone to reserve it.

If you want to take a taxi up to the beginning of the Arakawa trail,

each passenger has to buy a road usage ticket for ¥850 one way in addition to the fare.

There are three main taxi companies in Yakushima:

- **Matsubanda Koutsu** (まつばんだ交通タクシー) has offices in Miyanoura and Anbo ☎ 43-5000/43-5555 (12 taxis).

- **Yakushima Koutsu** (屋久島交通タクシー) is based in Miyanoura ☎ 42-0611, Anbo ☎ 46-2321 and in Onoaida ☎ 47-2081 (24 taxis)

- **Anbo Taxi** (安房タクシー) is only in Anbo ☎ 46-2311 (8 taxis).

HITCHHIKING

It is not an uncommon site to see hitchhikers around the coastal road and it is usually quite easy to get a ride, often with local people willing to be hospitable. It does depend on the time of day and the weather though as to how long you are by the roadside.

Stand just outside of the village on the road you want to go on and stick out your thumb. This is Yakushima and people are usually much friendlier than you would find in mainland cities however use the same caution you would elsewhere when accepting rides from strangers. Yakushima attracts all sorts of people as visitors – the good and the bad.

4 PRACTICALITIES

POST OFFICE

There are two main post offices (郵便局) on Yakushima, one in Anbo on the port turn-off, a short distance from Kagoshima Bank (鹿児島銀行), the other in the centre of Miyanoura - after Miyanoura bridge take a left and it is on your right. Both have ATM machines available (which will accept major credit cards). There are also smaller post offices, with limited facilities, in most of the other villages.

MONEY

Cash is still the only form of currency readily accepted in Yakushima. Credit or debit cards are not widely accepted outside of the big hotels.

BANKS

Kagoshima Bank (鹿児島銀行) and **Minami Nihon Bank** (南日本銀行) have branches in Miyanoura and Anbo. They have no facilities for currency exchange but have ATM machines which accept major credit cards, however card compatibility can be an issue.

INTERNET

Wi-Fi is available in some accommodations like both the youth hostels, Yakushima Green Hotel, Business Inn Yaedake and the JR Hotel but also at the following places:

• **Yakushima Kanko center** (屋久島観光センター) in Miyanoura.

• **Yakushima Messenger** (屋久島メッセンジャー) outdoor store in Koseda.

• **Yoronzaka cafe** (よろん坂) in Anbo (See advert in Food & Drink)

GAS STATIONS

There are no gas stations on the western side of the island between Kurio and Nagata. Gas stations are generally open from 08.30 to 19.00 but many are closed on weekends. In the larger villages like Anbo, Miyanoura and near the airport, gas stations are usually open at weekends (incl. Sundays) but most open according to a rota so the exact gas station which opens is changeable. 'Self' gas station in Koseda (next to Some's) is usually open when others are not. It is of course best if possible to fill up before Sunday to avoid wasting time searching.

SUPERMARKETS

Miyanoura area

• **Wai Wai Land** (わいわいランド) is opposite the hospital. ☼ 09.00 – 20.00 ☏ 42-2525.

• **A Co-op** (A コープ) is on the mountain road to Shiratani Unsuikyo.☼ 9.30 – 20.00 (19.00 in winter) ☏ 42-1000.

• **Life Centre Yakuden** (ライフセンターヤクデン) 200 m past Yakushima Environmental Culture Village Centre on the main road heading towards Nagata ☼ 09.00 – 21.00. ☏ 42-1501

All the above sell a wide selection of food and many other things like clothes, DIY equipment and furniture. Life Centre Yakuden also sells camping and fishing equipment.

Koseda area

• **Drugstore Mori** (ドラッグストアモリ) and **Drug eleven** (ドラッグイレブン) ① 49-4141 are two large drug stores and Drug eleven has a very useful ¥100 section ② 09.00 – 21.00.

• **Some's** (サムズ) ① 43-5963 is a hardware store selling a limited selection of food but mostly camping gear, fishing equipment, clothes and DIY ② 09.00 – 21.00.

• **M Mart** (エムマート) ① 43-5128 is on Route 77 in Koseda village ② 9.00- 20.00.

Anbo area

• **A Co-op** (A コープ) ① 49-7820 is within a building called 'Eco-Town Awaho' (エコタウンあわほ) with a handful of smaller stores. It is opposite the jet foil port and sells packed lunches and snacks as well as more general food. ② 09.30 – 20.00 (19.00 in winter).

• **Tanaka Seika** (田中青果・生花) ① 46-4567 is on Route 77 near the Green Hotel and is a general supermarket ② 08.30-20.00.

• **Shiba** (しいば) ① 46-2067 is just before the mountain road to Yakusugiland and is renowned for its freshly baked bread and cakes ② 07.00 – 20.00.

Onoaida area

• **A Co-op** (A コープ) ① 47-2611 is also in Onoaida near the main junction on the by-pass road. At the traffic signals turn towards Onoaida and the supermarket is on your right ② 09.00 – 20.00 (19.00 in winter).

• There is also a convenience store, **Ai shop** ① 47-2140 (アイショップはるやま) on the by-pass at the north end of the village.

Kurio area

• **S Mart** (S マート) ① 48-2805 convenience store is in the centre of Kurio and sells a wide selection of food and drink.

Isso area

• **Maruichi store** (丸一ストア) ① 44-2049 ② 08.00-19.00 in the centre of Isso.

BOOKSTORES

• **Tomari Shoten** (泊書店) ① 46-3111 has a bookshop in Anbo as the road bends down to the river, after the police station. They sell books, magazines and maps. ② 09.00 – 19.00.

• There is also a smaller bookshop in Miyanoura called **Flora** (フローラ) ① 42-0134, on the main street between the 2nd and 3rd traffic signals from the river.

TOURIST INFORMATION

There are centers in Miyanoura port building ① 42-1019, in Koseda ① 49-4010 near the entrance of the airport car park and in Anbo ① 46-2333 opposite Moss burger at the junction before Anbo Bridge. And in all no English is spoken!

LAUNDRY

There are 24-hour automated laundrettes in various locations around the island. There is one next to SOME'S hardware store in Koseda, in Miyanoura behind Yakuden store and near A co-op supermarket, and in Anbo next to You shop on the main road. These have washing machines, driers and specialist equipment like shoe washer/driers.

GARBAGE

There are very few public litter bins on the island and you are expected to carry whatever you use until you can dispose of it at your accommodation or other appropriate place.

POLICE

The main police station (屋久島警察署) is in Anbo, at the top of the hill on the main road leading down to the river. There are smaller stations in most of the villages. As with the rest of Japan, the emergency number to call for the police is **110**.

HOSPITALS & CLINICS

There is one main hospital on the island: **Yakushima Tokushukai** (屋久島徳州会病院) ① 42-2200. It is on the main coastal road in Miyanoura, opposite Wai Wai Land (わいわいランド) supermarket.

There are also smaller but well-equiped clinics in other larger villages:

- **Koseda Shinryojo** ① 43-5100 (小瀬田診療所) in Koseda.

- **Nakaiin** (仲医院) ① 46-2131 in Anbo.

- **Onoaida Shinryojo** ① 47-3277 (尾之間診療所) in Onoaida.

The emergency number for an ambulance is **119**.

COIN LOCKERS

Coin lockers to store your luggage are available at **Yakushima Kanko Centre** (屋久島観光センター) in Miyanoura ① 42-0091 and **Mori-no-kirameki** (森のきらめき) in Anbo ① 49-7101 🖳 morinokirameki.com

- Large 80 cm x 40 cm x 40 cm

- Small 40 cm x 40 cm x 40 cm

There are also facilities in **Furusatoichiba** (ふるさと市場) in Miyanoura and **Anbo Port**.

BAGGAGE FORWARDING

Yakushima Kanko Centre (屋久島観光センター) and **Furusatoichiba** (ふるさと市場) in Miyanoura and **Mori-no-kirameki** (森のきらめき) in Anbo, will also send your bags on to anywhere on the island. This could be very convenient if you are crossing the mountains and want to stay the other side of the island. The cost is normally ¥300 per item.

5 FOOD & DRINK

Most visitors stay in accommodation which includes evening meals and where possible it is usually the best option as it gives you the chance to taste home cooked Yakushima food. If not, there is a selection of places to eat, although the range of food is somewhat limited.

PACKED LUNCHES (弁当)

It is common for hikers to reserve a freshly cooked packed lunch before they go hiking in Yakushima. Should you wish to do the same, you need to order the food the day before and collect it on the way to the mountain in the early hours of the morning. The pick-up time should be arranged when ordering. You can usually order this through your accommodation but here are the main stores that provide this service:

Miyanoura area

Shimamusubi (島むすび) ☎ 42-0770, **Yaohachi** (八百八) ☎ 42-4007 or **Attaka Bento** (あったか弁当) ☎ 42-3222.

Anbo area

Asahi Bento (あさひ弁当) ☎ 46-4007 or **Dekitateya** (できたて屋) ☎ 46-3071

Alternatively if you are happy to pick up a packed lunch on the colder side, A co-op (A コープ) or Wai Wai land (わいわいランド) have a large selection and are often discounted later in the day.

BAKERIES

Miyanoura area

For cakes try **Shingetsudo** (新月堂菓子舗) ☎ 42-0131 next to Minami Nihon Bank (南日本銀行) in the centre of Miyanoura or for homemade bread and other bakery products try **Kimuraya** (木村屋) ☎ 42-0453 after Miyanoura bridge on the left or **Hiramiya** (凡我堂 ひらみ屋) ☎ 42-2056 opposite Yakushima high school (屋久島高校) up the hill (towards Anbo) from Miyanoura river.

Anbo area

Shiiba (しいば) is close to, and on the same side as, the turn off for Yakusugiland again on Route 77. It offers a wide selection of bread, sandwiches and cakes. ☎ 46-2067

Onoaida area

Peita (ペイタ) sells fresh bread and cakes. It is in the centre of Onoaida 200 m on the road leading to the JR hotel. ☺ 9.00-18.00. Closed Tues. ☎ 47-3166.

WESTERN FOOD/CAFES

Miyanoura area

• **Rest in Yakushima** (レストイン 屋久島) is in the Yakushima Kanko Centre (屋久島観光センター), a two-floored lime green building close to the entrance of the port. ☺ 08.30-17.00 ☎ 42-0091

• **Gurosu Curry House** (グロース) is located next to Miyanoura River opposite the small river-side rest area. ☎ 080-2710-1572. See ad for more details.

CURRY, PIZZA & SHOCHU BAR

Open 11am-3pm & 6pm-4am

グロース

CURRY HOUSE 屋久島町宮之浦48-2

080-2710-1572

• **Restaurant Teradaya**（レストラン 洋食寺田屋）is on the main road in Miyanoura opposite another listed restaurant, Yakiniku Ippudo. It is midway between Miyanoura River and the Port on the sea side of the main road and serves set meals. ☺ 11.00-14.00 & 17.30-21.00. Closed Sat. ☏ 49-1117 🖥 teradaya.ecnet.jp

• **Mam's Kitchen** (屋久島まむずきっ ちん) is at the Elementary school/ mountain road junction near Miyanoura bridge. Fresh home-made hamburgers from ¥450. ☺ 11.00-18.00. Closed Mon. ☏ 42-2822

Koseda area

• **Il Mare**（イルマーレ）serves authentic Italian food in form of pizza, pasta and set menus. On Route 77, 100 m north of the airport in Koseda. ☺ 11.30-14.30 & 18.00-20.30. ☏ 43-5666 🖥 ilmare3.jp

• **Kissa Jurin**（喫茶樹林）Good for light meals (toast, salad, coffee etc). Head from the airport towards Miyanoura and turn left just before 'au' & Some's store, it is 100 m from the turn off. ☺ 10.00-18.00. Closed Sun. ☏ 43-5454 🖥 jurinn.com

• **Aikotei**（あいこ亭）has its own entrance within the Airport Hotel （屋久島エアポートホテル）next to the airport. Has various set meals for lunch and dinner including steak. ☺ 11.30-14.00 & 17.00-20.30. ☏ 43-5788

• **La Monstera**（ラ モンステラ）serves stuffed rice omelettes with home-farmed eggs. It is a short way from the airport on the sea side of the main road (Anbo direction), close to the lighthouse. Only open 11.30am-3pm on Thurs, Frid & Sat. ☏ 43-5080 🖥 qx-et.co.jp/Yakushima

• **Hibiscus**（ハイビスカス）serves curry in many shapes and forms – seafood, hamburger, cutlet, vegetable etc. It is close to La Monstera above on the sea side of the main road south from Koseda. ☏ 43-5195 🖥 www9.ocn.ne.jp/ ~haibi/

Anbo area

• **Yoronzaka**（よろん坂）is on the mountain side of the hill heading south out of Anbo. It has free Wi-Fi and is a café at lunchtime and a bar at night. Very friendly, very relaxed and a warm welcome to foreign visitors. ☏ 46-2949 ☺ 11.00-23.00 🖥 yoronzaka.yakushima.ch

• **Restaurant San Paulo**（レストラン サンパウロ）is a 'family restaurant' with a wide selection of set meals and their own brand of salad dressing. It is close to Anbo jet foil port, 200 m down the hill from the post office. ☺ 10.00-15.00 & 17.30-22.00. Closed 1st & 3rd Tues of the

month. ☎ 46-3848
💻 www12.ocn.ne.jp/~sanpauro

• **Smiley** (スマイリー) makes their own cakes and sandwiches in a small cafe by Anbo river. Signed on the river road between the fishing port and Anbo bridge. 🕐 11.00-18.00. Closed on Tues. ☎ 46-2853 💻 plaza.rakuten.co.jp/yakushimasmiley

Hirauchi area

• **Kaisenchaya** (喫茶海泉茶屋) Serves set meals (meat cutlets and deep fried shrimp) in cosy surroundings. At No.110 Nishikaikon (西開墾) bus stop in Hirauchi take the small turning towards the sea and it is 100 m on the right. 🕐 11.00-15.00. Closed Mon ☎ 47-3322.

Nagata area

• **Mam's Kitchen** (屋久島まむずきっちん) offers 'healthy' light meals including tofu burgers, curry and salads. It is part of Yakushima Tsuwanoya hotel (屋久島 つわのや) and is 1 km towards Seibu Rindo from Nagata and signed on the sea side of the main road. 🕐 11.30-16.00. Last orders for lunch at 14.30. Closed Thurs and Sun. ☎ 45-2717 💻 tsuwanoya.com

JAPANESE/CHINESE FOOD

Many in the following list are small, local restaurants who probably speak little English but Yakushima

is a friendly place and perfect for trying traditional food.

Miyanoura area

• **Furusatoichiba** (ふるさと市場) has a wide selection of food and is a good choice if you are not sure what food to eat. They serve flying fish and Yakushima food as well as noodles and rice dishes. It is opposite the park at the entrance to the port. The front section is a large souvenir shop but the back section is a restaurant with solid yakusugi tables. 🕐 19.30 – 21.00. ☎ 42-3333 💻 yakushima.co.jp/ichiba

• **Shiosai** (潮騒) Serves Japanese food and has a good reputation for its seafood. It is on the sea side of the main road in Miyanoura closer to the port entrance than the river. Closed Thurs. ☎ 42-2721.

• **Ebisudaikoku Toshi** (恵比寿大黒としし) serves traditional Japanese set meals. Turn inland at Miyanoura river [Miyanoura centre side] and take the next right. 🕐 17.00-22.30 ☎ 42-0461

• **Kaedean** (楓庵) Serves Japanese noodles (soba and udon) near Nakagawa Sports store on the main road in Miyanoura, midway between the river and the port entrance. Closed Sun. ☎ 42-0398.

• **Yakiniku Ippudo** (焼肉一風堂) is a large restaurant serving yakiniku

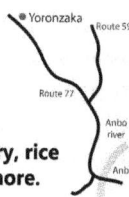

(fried meat that you cook yourself on a flat plate at your table). It is midway between Miyanoura river and the Port on the sea side of the main road in a traditional building. Look for the orange signs. ⏰ 11.00-14.00 & 17.00-22.00. Closed Wed. ☎ 42-1220.

• **Sushi Wakashio** (鮨若潮) serves locally caught sushi. It is in the centre of Miyanoura, one street inland from Nakagawa Sports on Route 77. ⏰ 17.00 – 22.00. Closed Tues. ☎ 42-2114

• **Ryuhou** (龍鳳) offers Chinese food like noodles and fried rice. It is at the end of the main pedestrian road parallel to the river, at the opposite end to the two banks, and close to the shrine. Closed on Sun. ⏰ 11.00–14.00 & 18.00–21.00. 💻 www7a.biglobe.ne.jp/~ryuhou ☎ 42-0825

• **Wanron** (王龍) is a small but very popular Chinese restaurant serving ramen noodles, fried rice and gyoza (fried dumplings). There are pictures of the menu on the wall to choose from. Serves black pork ramen (黒豚角煮ラーメン), a local dish. It is opposite Miyanoura Elementary school just before the river (from Anbo direction). ⏰ 11.00-21.00 ☎ 42-1222 💻 geocities.jp/wanron_yakushima/frame.html

Anbo area

• **Yakudon** (屋久どん) serves a good selection of local Yakushima food such as flying fish. Very popular and scenic setting by the sea. Close to Anbo port, follow the road past

A co-op and it is on the sea side of the road after the car park and toilets. ⏰ 10.00-21.00 ☎ 46-3210 💻 yakushima-net.com/restaurant.html

• **Hanasatuki** (花皐月) offers yakiniku and a selection of local food. Turn inland at the junction after the Green Hotel (coming from Miyanoura direction) and it is 100 m on the right. ☎ 46-3293 💻 www2.ocn.ne.jp/~hanastk

• **Sushi Isonokaori** (寿司 いその香り) is a popular restaurant serving sushi and sashimi on the mountain side of Route 77 on the way into Anbo from Miyanoura. ⏰ 11.30-14.00 & 18.00-22.00. Closed Tues. ☎ 46-3218

• **Banraiken** (萬来軒) is a busy Chinese restaurant with large servings. It specialises in 'ramen' noodles but also has a section offering sushi. It is a few doors away from Anbo post office up the hill from the port. ⏰ 11.00-15.00 & 17.30-21.30 ☎ 46-2109. Closed every 2nd Thursday.

• **Nodoka** (のどか) offers set meals for lunch. Turn left at the top of the hill heading south out of Anbo at Kobayashi Kogeisho (小林工芸所) workshop and look for the small sign. ⏰ 11.00-15.00. Closed Thurs. ☎ 46-2669.

• **Michikusa** (みち草) is a very small local restaurant serving traditional food such as Yakushima black pork cutlets (黒豚カツ). It is next to Kashima Kougei (鹿島工芸) on the hill leading out of Anbo (Onoaida direction). Closed Mon. ☎ 46-2670

- **Sugi-no-chaya** (杉の茶屋) serves light meals like noodles and rice balls for lunch. It has a rustic setting in the forest in the grounds of the Yakusugi museum. ⏰ 10.00-14.00. Closed the first Tues every month. ☎ 46-2484 💻 eco-festa.jp/suginochaya

- **Kirankuya** (きらんくや) serves Japanese noodles. It is on the small road that leads behind A co-op. Go under the bridge and it is at the end. Closed on Tues. ☎ 46-4610.

Onoaida area

- **Daimon** (大門) serves a wide selection of Chinese food. It is on the road that leads to the JR hotel opposite the post office. ⏰ 11.00-14.30 & 17.30-20.30. ☎ 47-2050.

- **Fuan** (風庵) is a small restaurant serving Japanese noodles (Udon). Take the first turn off to Onoaida from the main road (from Anbo direction). Turn left straight after MOKU restaurant and at the next junction turn right. It is then 300 m ahead. ⏰ 11.30-14.00 for lunch or 10.00-17.00 as a cafe. Closed Tues. ☎ 47-3955.

Hirauchi area

- **Hachiman** (はちまん) serves seafood and a set menu during the day. Opposite the turning to Hachiman Elementary School (八幡小学校) on the main road in Hirauchi. Open 11.00 – 14.00 & 18.00 – 23.00. Closed on Tues. ☎ 47-2888.

Kurio area

- **Shochiku** (松竹) is a very traditional restaurant which offers handmade Soba noodles. At the junction before Kurio bridge turn inland towards Kurio Elementary school (栗生小学校) and it is on your right. Look for the wooden lantern on the wall. ☎ 48-2323.

Nagata area

- **Jyaraitei** (じゃらい亭) serves traditional Yakushima dishes like black pork cutlets (黒豚カツ) and flying fish (トビウオ) as well as more typical Japanese food. From No.2 Nagata Iriguchi (永田入口) bus stop head towards the mountains and look for the sign on the building. ⏰ 11.00-14.00 (Oct-April) & 18.00-23.00. Closed Mon. ☎ 45-2078.

IZAKAYA (居酒屋)

Izakaya are bars, pubs and small restaurants all mixed into one and are good places to have a drink and to eat. There are many on Yakushima but here are a popular selection.

Miyanoura area

- **Izakaya Ganta** (居酒屋 がん太) is located by Miyanoura River and is popular with a cross section of people. Food is standard Izakaya fayre but also has flying fish. Closed on the 1st and 3rd Sunday of the month. Closes at 11.30 pm.

- **Meshiya Tenten** (めし屋 天天) is a popular small izakaya and is on the main road just past the second traffic signals from Miyanoura bridge (heading Nagata direction). It is on the right. ☎ 42-0689.

Anbo area

• **Yoronzaka** (よろん坂) – see the café section and the ad. Highly recommended purely for the great characters who run it. Free Wi-Fi ☎ 46-2949 ⏰ 11.00-23.00 💻 yoronzaka.yakushima.ch

• **St.Poté** (散歩亭) is a modern Izakaya run by young staff with a wide selection of food and music. There is a cosy back section often playing jazz. It has a fantastic riverside setting near Manten bridge (まんてん橋), the old Anbo bridge, on the opposite side of the river. ⏰ 18.00-1.00 ☎ 46-2905 💻 www17.ocn.ne.jp/~stpote

• **Burari** (風来り) is a friendly little Izakaya further along the road next to Moss Burger. Continue until the end and it is on the right, opposite Kashima Business Hotel. Closed Wed. ☎ 46-2111.

• **Ajidokoro Furusato** (味処 ふるさと) is on the small road leading to Manten bridge (the older of the two bridges) in Anbo centre. ⏰ 17.00 – 22.00. Closed every 2nd Thurs. ☎ 46-3506

• **Youfu Izakaya Tsubone** (洋風居酒屋つぼね) is a modern Isakaya also very close to Manten Bridge in Anbo centre. From the bridge go straight and it is on the left amongst the small stores. Closed Sun. ☎ 46-2116.

Hirauchi area

• **Hachiman** (はちまん) is in the restaurant section but also functions as an izakaya at night. Opposite the turning to Hachiman Elementary School (八幡小学校) on the main road in Hirauchi. ⏰ until 22.00. Closed on Tues. ☎ 47-2888.

FOOD AND DRINK SPECIALITIES OF YAKUSHIMA

While in Yakushima there are many types of food to try which can only be found on the island or in this area of Japan. The following is a list of popular Yakushima delicacies:

Citrus fruit	• **Tankan** (たんかん) are harvested between Feb-March and are a cross between a ponkan and an orange. They are thought to be juicier and sweeter. A box of 15 of either is ¥2,000 and 1 bag at road side shop is ¥200. You can also buy Tankan/Ponkan squeezed juice and ice cream or sorbet.
	• **Ponkan** (ぽんかん) are harvested from December. They are softer than tankan and have a richer taste.
Rice/ potato	• **Kakaran dango** (かからん団子) is a sticky rice cake made with yomogi (Japanese mugwort) wrapped with a china root leaf. ¥300 for 4.
	• **Yakutoro** (屋久とろ) are Yam potatoes which are grown in Yakushima. 1 bag for ¥100-200.
Flying fish	• **Kubioresaba** (首折れさば). 'Saba' means mackerel and 'Kubiore' means broken neck. They are so named because as soon as they are caught, their necks are broken to keep them fresh.

They can be eaten as raw sashimi or in shabushabu, a boiled stew. The whole fish can be bought for ¥800 at the supermarket and you can ask them to make it into sashimi for free.

• **Tsukeage** (つけ揚げ) is a deep fried Tobiuo (flying fish) fish cake. It costs ¥130 for one Yakuage at Yakushima Kanko Centre restaurant in Miyanoura.

• **Tobiuo no Karaage** (飛び魚の唐揚げ) is deep fried Tobiuo fish which soaked in light salted water for a night.

• **Tobiuo no ichiyaboshi** (飛び魚の一夜干し) is tobiuo fish which has been dried for the night after soaked in salty water. It costs around ¥450.

Shell-fish

• **Tokobushi** (とこぶし) or **Isomon** (いそもん) are small abalone and caught at low tide every month. You can see local people scouring the rocks for them with net bags and hooked spears.

• **Kame-no-te** (かめのて) is a shellfish known as 'Se' and is found in April-June. It has the appearance of a turtle's hand hence the name 'kame-no-te' (Turtle's hand).

Drinks

• **Passion wine** (パッションワイン) is red or white wine made with locally grown passion fruit. ¥950 a bottle

(720ml).

• **Mitake shochu** (三岳 焼酎) is a distilled alcohol made from sweet potatoes with around 25% alcohol by volume. It is the most popular brand of shochu in Yakushima and when deliveries of the large ¥2,000 bottles arrive in supermarkets, lines form and only one purchase per person is allowed.

6 ACCOMMODATION

There is a wide variety of accommodation on Yakushima from top of the range hotels to basic mountain huts and to help you find the best place to stay, I have narrowed down the choices in the following sections. If you wish to stay in the free mountain huts you will find more details of them in the hiking section.

NOTE: Japanese accommodation names reveal what kind of accommodation is offered.

 • **Hotel** (ホテル): A modern hotel resembling those in the West.

 • **Ryokan** (旅館): A traditional inn, serving traditional food, with tatami rooms.

 • **Pension** (ペンション): A small modern guest house.

 • **Minshuku** (民宿): A converted house, rooms are usually tatami mat and traditional.

 • **Sudomari Minshuku** (素泊まり民宿): Similar to a minshuku but does not serve food and has a kitchen at your disposal instead.

Prices range from ¥1,700 to ¥18,000 but within these wide price bands there is a whole host of different services offered by each accommodation so make sure you read the individual details of each entry. The list here is selective and there are many perfectly good places which did not make this guide but I have tried to include a broad mixture of accommodation based on good service and reputation.

Often prices are based on breakfast and dinner included and the price can be reduced if you opt not to have your meals at the accommodation but be aware that outside of the main villages you may need your own transport to find a restaurant. The list is organised by location.

Miyanoura area

 • **Oceanview Campsite** (オーシャンビューキャンプ場) is on the south side of the river. Turn towards the sea at Miyanoura Elementary school and turn right before the port. Camping is ¥800 pp/n and 5-person tents can be for ¥5,000 and 4-person for ¥4,000. ☎ 42-0091 💻 y-ovc.com

 • **Kairakuen Campsite & Minshuku** (民宿海楽園キャンプ場) is close to No.33 Eidan (営団) bus stop. Turn towards the sea at Miyanoura hospital (屋久島徳州会病院) and continue to the end (the cliff top). Camping is ¥800 pp/n, ¥100 for a shower and rental bungalows for ¥1,200 pp/n. The minshuku is from ¥3,500 pp/n without meals. ☎ 42-0269 💻 e-yakushima.jp

 • ☺ **Port side Youth Hostel** (ポートサイドユースホステル) is conveniently placed near the centre of Miyanoura but not in the prettiest of places. At the port entrance there is a park with toilets and picnic tables. Follow the road that runs at the other side of the park to the port. The youth hostel is a short walk on the left. Free internet. From ¥3,540 pp/n ☎ 49-1316 🖳 yakushima-yh.net

• **Yaedake Minshuku** (民宿八重 岳) ☎ 42-1551 (Lodge) 42-2552 (Minshuku) is on Route 77 in the centre of Miyanoura on the right just before the second traffic signals after the river. They also have lodges at **Lodge Yaedakesanso** (ロッジ八重岳山荘). These are near the river and consist of comfortable wooden cabins connected by raised walkways in the forest. Free use of canoes and hammocks. From ¥6,000 pp/n. When you book, make sure you specify lodge or minshuku. 🖳 http://www17.ocn.ne.jp/~yakusima/lodge/index.html

• **Seaside Hotel Yakushima** (シーサイドホテル屋久島) is a large older hotel close to the port with its entrance before you reach the Yakushima Environmental Culture Village Centre from the port terminal. It is popular with tour groups. From ¥13,650 pp/n. ☎ 42-0175 🖳 www.ssh-yakushima.co.jp ✉ yoyaku@ssh-yakushima.co.jp

Kusugawa area

• **Kusugawa Mae-dake campsite** (楠川前岳キャンプ場) is in Kusugawa and offers rental barbecue, free

washing machine and cold showers. Tents ¥700 pp/n, ¥2,500 room only. Seasonal - call ahead. ☎ 42-2120

• **Hanagoyomi Sudomari Minshuku** (素泊まり民宿 花ごよみ) has a good reputation and its own garden with a walking path. It is on the sea side of the road between Kusugawa and Koseda on Route 77. From ¥2,500 without meals but offers use of a kitchen. ☎ 42-1838 🖳 www.hanagoyomi.ecnet.jp

• ☺ **Holiday House** (ホリデー ハウス) is just before Otoko River (男川) and north of Fureai Park (ふれあいパーク) rest area. The bus stop is No.42 Otoko-gawa (男川). Run by a delightful couple who speak English. From ¥3,500 not including meals. ☎ 43-5047 (See ad) ✉ holiday-house@alpha.ocn.ne.jp

• **Shiratani Minshuku** (民宿白谷) is in Kusugawa, coming from Miyanoura take the last left before the river and it is on the corner. It has a rock bath hut with sea views. From ¥6,500 with two meals. ☎ 42-0809 🖳 www3.ocn.ne.jp/~siratani ✉ shiratani@wonder.ocn.ne.jp

Koseda area

• **Rider house Tomarigi** (ライダー ハウスとまり木) is close to the airport in Koseda. At the airport junction turn inland and go along the small road that runs next to Manten (まんてん). Friendly and

very relaxed atmosphere with Wi-Fi. From ¥2,000 and you can pitch a tent for ¥800. ☎ 43-5069 🖥 yakushima-tomarigi.jp

• **Airport Hotel** (エアポートホテル) is a business hotel quite literally next to the airport with a popular restaurant called 'Aikotei' (あいこ亭). Single room - ¥5,500 without meals, twin - ¥10,500. 🖥 homepage2.nifty.com/yakushima-aph ☎ 43-5551 FAX 43-5530

• **Yakutetsu Campsite** (キャンプ 場 ヤクテツ) is located beside the river in between Koseda village and the airport and signed inland on the main road. By bus get off at No.44 Koseda (小瀬田) bus stop and walk down the hill in the direction of the airport (South-East). It is then a right turn after the small river. It has a shower and covered cooking area. ¥800 pp/n for adults and ¥500 for children. ☎ 43-5144

• **Jomon-no-yado Manten** (縄文の宿まんてん) is a resort hotel right across the road from the airport. It boasts an onsen and buffet restaurant. From ¥12,500 pp/n. ☎ 43-5751 🖥 www.arm-manten.co.jp

Funayuki area

• **Passion Kan** (パッション館) is signed inland from the main road. Get off at No.57 Kuwano (桑野) bus stop and take the road inland for 5 min before turning left. It offers a

free tour to Oko-no-taki, the seaside Onsens and Gajyumaru trees in Autumn. From ¥4,000 pp/n. Also has an annex with a kitchen for ¥3,000 pp/n. ☎ 46-2744 🖥 www5.ocn.ne.jp/~yakuview/passion

• ☺ **Mori-no-kokage** (森のこかげ) is signed on the main road just north of Anbo. Turn towards the sea and it is 100 m on the left. Run by a welcoming English speaker, it offers clean homemade wooden cabins, free use of a hammock to hang on the porch and barbecue facilities. Great attention to detail From ¥4,250 pp/n ☎ 9060017512 (See ad on back cover) 🖥 oshirase@morinokokage.net 🖥 morinokokage.net (English)

Anbo area

• **Banyamine Campsite** (番屋峯 キャンプ場) is beside Yakudon (屋久どん) restaurant overlooking the harbour in Anbo. From the jet foil port turn right, go past A co-op (on your left) and after the parking area with toilets (on your right) turn right down to a collection of buildings by the sea. The campsite is at the end of these buildings, the last one of which is Yakudon restaurant. Tents and camping equipment can be rented. ⏰ all year round. ¥500 pp/n + tent price from ¥200. Shower for ¥500 (20 min). ☎ 46-3210 FAX 46-2955 🖥 yakushima-net.com/camp.html

• **Hanasatsuki** (花皐月) is near Anbo Elementary School (安房小学校). Turn towards the mountains at the large hall and police station (屋久島警察署) and then take the second right. It is on this road after a few minutes. From ¥3,150 pp/n or if you have a sleeping bag ¥2,000 pp/n. ☎ 46-3687/ 09095668517 ▣ hanasatuki.9123@vega.ocn.ne.jp

• **Backpackers House** (素泊まり民宿 ゆかいな仲間たち) is above Moss burger near the river. Conveniently placed basic dorms. ¥2,500 p/n + ¥200 to rent a blanket. ☎ + FAX 46-3661 ▣ www1.ocn.ne.jp/~t.m106

• **Mori-no-kirameki** (森のきらめき) is on Route 77 at the junction at the top of the hill in the centre of Anbo. Downstairs is an outdoors store and upstairs is Conveni-lodge (コンビニロッジ) which consists of en-suite dorms with clean wooden bunks. From ¥3,200 pp/n. ▣ morinokirameki.com ☎ 49-7101

• **Daichan House** (大ちゃんハウス) offers rooms in authentic Mongol huts. It is on Route 77 heading south out of Anbo. Climb the long hill and at the very top as it bends, look for the sign on the left. Has very good reviews – clean rooms and very friendly owners. From ¥3,150 pp/n. ☎ + FAX 46-3565 ▣ www.tochinoki.com/daichan

• **Suimeiso Minshuku** (民宿 水明荘) sits beside Anbo River, further inland than Manten Bridge (まんてん橋). It is on the second road up, running parallel to the north side of the river. Japanese film director Hayao Miyazaki is reputed to love this minshuku. From ¥3,500 pp/n without meals and ¥6,800 with two meals. ☎ 46-2078 ▣ plaza.rakuten.co.jp/suimeisou ▣ suimeisou@gmail.com

• **Takenko Minshuku** (民宿 たけんこ) is renowned for good food and clean rooms. Turn towards the mountain from Route 77 at the first traffic signals as you come into Anbo (from Miyanoura direction). There is a gas station on one corner. Go straight and as the road bends sharply to the left, turn right. It is soon after on your left. From ¥5,500 pp/n with two meals. ☎ 46-3382 ▣ www17.plala.or.jp/takenko

• ☺ **Tabibito-no-yado Manmaru** (旅人の宿 まんまる) has rooms laid out motel style around an open

area and at one end a large communal bath, the other the restaurant. Very friendly with some English spoken and close to the port. Follow the road running behind A co-op, go through the short tunnel and it is on the left. From ¥5,500. ① 45-2137 ⌨ manmaru.jimdo.com (English)

• **Oyado Tsuruya** (御宿 鶴屋) is very close to the jet foil port in Anbo, a short way along the main road from A co-op. It is famous for its traditional Yakushima food. From ¥8,400 pp/n with two meals. Book online for ¥500 discount ① 46-2120 ⌨ yakushima-turuya.jp

• **Yakushima Green Hotel** (屋久島グリーンホテル) is on Route 77 at the north end of Anbo. It has a spa with a hot stone massage and an artificially heated onsen. From ¥10,500 pp/n. ① 46-3021 ⌨ yakushima-gh.com/index.html

Takahira area

• **Shizen-no-yado Tennenmura** (自然の宿 天然村) is a traditional 7 room guesthouse hidden away on the mountain. Get off at No.83 Takahira (高平) bus stop and it is a 15 min walk towards the mountains on the narrow windy road. It is signed from Route 77 and there are more signs as you go up, one of which will tell you to turn left. It is then a short walk further on and it is on the right.

The main attraction here is that it serves only organic and vegetarian food and will cater to other diets if requested. From ¥6,300 pp/n. ① & FAX 47- 2541 ⌨ tennen-mura@i-next.ne.jp

Mugio area

• **Cottage HANAMANA** (コテージ HANAMANA) offers luxurious country-style rooms on the mountain side. By car turn towards the mountain just south of Mugio or get off at No.86 Botanical Research Park bus stop, follow the sign to Senpiro waterfall (千尋の滝) heading inland for about 200 m and then turn left at the pink sign. Offers peaceful surroundings, an open air bath and the possibility to charter the whole house. From ¥9,500 pp/n ① & FAX 47-3398 ✉ catseye@lily.odn.ne.jp ⌨ hanamana.org

Hara area

• **Iyashi no yado TonTon** 癒しの宿とんとん) has a spa offering body massage, reflexology and hand massage. Take the next left after the bridge over Toroki falls (coming from Anbo direction). The nearest bus stop is No.88 Hara Iriguchi (原入口). From ¥8,500. ① 49-3560 ⌨ homepage3.nifty.com/ton-ton ✉ iyashi-tonton@nifty.com

Onoaida area

• ☺ **Chinryu-An** (枕流庵) is a small, friendly guest house south of

Onoaida, very used to foreigners and with English spoken. It is at No.101 Yaishi (矢石) bus stop heading out of Onoaida to Hirauchi. From ¥5,100 pp/n including meals and ¥3,900 without. Also offers rental gear and bicycles. ① 47-3900 ✉ yakushima@chinryu.com 🖳 chinryu.com (English)

• ☺ **Shikinoyado Onoaida** (四季の宿尾之間) is conveniently situated just after the large red sign of the man in the Hawaiian shirt on Route 77, turn right (coming from Anbo direction). Has an organic garden and very friendly and welcoming owner who speaks good English. From ¥8,500 pp/n. ① 47-3377 🖳 h3.dion.ne.jp/~yasuakim/ english.html (English) ✉ yasuakim@f8.dion.ne.jp

• ☺ **JR Hotel Yakushima** (ＪＲホテル屋久島) has panoramic sea/mountain views from its cliff-top location, its own onsen and the rooms have internet access. In the centre of Onoaida and signed from the main road. From ¥13,000 pp/n for a twin. ① 47-2011 🖳 jrhotelgroup.com/eng/ hotel/eng154.htm (English)

• ☺ **Yakushima Iwasaki Hotel** (屋久島いわさきホテル) is an impressive

hotel with a tree growing in the lobby, its own waterfall path and its own shuttle bus to Miyanoura port and Yakushima airport. It can be seen rising out of the forest west of Onoaida and has its own turn off just outside of the village, heading towards Hirauchi. From ¥22,000 ① 47-3888 🖳 yakushima.iwasakihotels.com/en/index.php (English)

Hirauchi area

• ☺ **Yakushima Youth hostel** (屋久島ユースホステル) is just north of Hirauchi village and is signed on the main road. By bus get off at No.107 Hirauchi Iriguchi (平内入口) bus stop. It offers camping on raised wooden platforms as well as dorms and rooms in the main youth hostel building. The setting is fairly isolated but Hirauchi seaside onsen (平内海中温泉) is nearby. ⊙ all year round. From ¥4,620 pp/n (¥3,540 without dinner) or camping ¥840 pp/n. ① 47-3751 🖳 yakushima-yh.net

Kurio area

• **Yakushima Youth Travel Village** (屋久島青少年旅行村) is on the west side of Kurio river. Cross the bridge and head up the hill towards Oko-

no-taki. It has facilities for camping (showers/ toilets/covered cooking area/washing machines) and a flat grass area for tents and also a section in the trees. Tents, cooking equipment, firewood and blankets can be rented. ¥420 pp/n for adults and ¥315 per child (under 6). There are also 9 rental bungalows with aircon/kitchen from ¥12,600 for 4 people. Close to the beach and Tsukasaki tide pool. ☉ April 1st to Oct 31st. ☎ 48-2871

Nagata area

• **Nagata Inakahama Campsite** （永田いなか浜キャンプ場） Positioned right on Inakahama beach （永田いなか浜） near the turtle watching areas and signed from the main road. The site is between No.5 Nakanobashi （中野橋） and No.6 Nakanoguchi （中野口） bus stops on the main coastal road. Opened

seasonally and from ¥800 per night. ☎ 45-2155 / 090 5027 6491

• **Yakushima Tsuwanoya** （屋久島つわのや） in Nagata has a restaurant and an artificial open-air bath. It is signed 1 km on the main road heading to Seibo Rindo. From ¥12,000 pp/n with two meals. ☎ + FAX 45-2717 🖥 tsuwanoya.com ✉ info@tsuwanoya.com

• **Soyoutei** （送陽邸） is a beautiful set of traditional buildings sat the far end of Inagahama beach. It has a very exclusive feel to it and you can eat and take a private bath directly overlooking the sea. There is also a private covered hammock area to swing away your stresses. Often featured in glossy magazines about Yakushima. From ¥12,600 pp/n. 🖥 soyote.ftw.jp/u44579.html ☎ + FAX 45-2819

7 HIKING IN THE MOUNTAINS

Hiking on Yakushima covers some of the best walking paths in Japan and are highly rated from casual walkers to serious climbers. There are several trails leading from the coast which are usually more demanding but there are also trails which start further into the inland mountains and even the most challenged walker can find a suitable path to enjoy the forest.

SHORT HIKES

If hiking is not really your thing but you would like to see some of the forest and the old Yakusugi trees, then **Yakusugiland** is ideal and gives a choice of trails from sturdy wooden platforms to scrambling on all fours. **Shiratani Unsuikyo** also offers a variety of trails and the chance to see one of the mountain huts. Another simpler hike is the Onoaida trail to **Janokuchi waterfall** from Onoaida Onsen, which being on the coast can be a good choice if cloud is covering the mountains, although even here there are a few steep sections.

Shorter day trips can be made taking the Yodogawa trail only as far as the sweeping views from the top of **Kuroimi dake** or take the trail to **Tachu dake** from Yakusugiland. There are also three short but challenging trails from the coast which climb lower but equally impressive mountains: **Aiko dake** from near Koseda offers panoramic 360° views; **Mochomu dake** from near Hara offers a dramatic view of the granite mountains and the coast; and the **Ryujinsugi trail** from Miyanoura leads through thick forest to rarely visited Yakusugi. These are often overlooked and well worth the climb.

LONG HIKES

Most people who visit want to see Jomon Sugi and take the **Arakawa trail** which, although not technically difficult to walk on, is a long, tiring path to complete in a day (a 9-10 hour round trip). Many also want to scale Miyanoura dake, the highest mountain in Southern Japan, and take the higher **Yodogawa trail** for another long day trip.

Some of the hardier hikers combine the trails and cross the island, spending the night in some of the 6 mountains huts. A popular route is to climb up through Shiratani Unsuikyo (Shiratani hut) and meet the Arakawa trail which then transforms into the Okabu trail to Jomon Sugi (Takatsuka hut or Shin Takatsuka hut). After Jomon sugi the Miyanoura trail allows a short diversion to the summit of Nagata dake (Shikanosawa hut) before the ascent to Miyanoura dake and then the Yodogawa path brings you via Hana-no-ego marsh (Ishizuka hut or Yodogawa hut) to the Yodogawa trail entrance and transport back down to Anbo. It is also popular to take the same trail combination in reverse as the descent from Miyanoura to Jomon sugi is much easier than the ascent.

There is a selection of other trails such as the Nagata trail, Yodogawa trail, Kurio trail, Onoaida trail, Yudomari trail and the Hanayama trail all of which offer another level of hiking and with the right equipment, preparation and state of mind, offers the serious hiker a real challenge.

HIKING EQUIPMENT

To enjoy your time safely on any of the mountain trails, it is highly recommended that you have at least the following equipment:

A pair of boots with a firm grip and protection for your ankles, water-proof rain gear, a hiking map, a compass, a flashlight and spare batteries, enough basic food provisions for your journey, a water container, a towel, gloves, a long-sleeved shirt, toilet paper and a backpack to put it all in.

Of course if you intend to stay in the huts, you will need a lot more. Including cooking equipment and a sleeping bag and outside of the summer you will need extra clothes to keep warm. A mobile is also a useful addition as at various points in the mountains, reception is good enough to make a call (from the top of Miyanoura dake, Nagata dake and the surrounding peaks, at some points on the trail to Jomon Sugi and the general rule of thumb - anywhere where you can see Tanegashima island).

A good hiking map to buy is the 'Yakushima/Miyanoura dake' map from the 'Yama-to-kogen chizu' series (山と高原地図屋久島宮之浦岳). It can be bought widely in Japan and online and is also available in Yakushima. There are no English translations but if used with this guide or a tourist map, it is very easy to follow.

If you arrived without much of the above but would like to take a mountain trail you are in luck because just about anything related to the mountains can be rented or bought in several stores on Yakushima.

RENTAL EQUIPMENT

Miyanoura area

• **Nakagawa Sports** (ナカガワ スポーツ) All kinds of mountain gear from rain wear, hiking boots and backpacks to dried food and repellent. ◯ 9.00-19.00. Closed on Wed. ◯ 42-0341 ▢ yakushima-

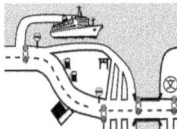

sp.com

• **Yakushima Kanko Centre**（屋久島観光センター）A wide variety of mountain gear and marine sports equipment. ⏲ 8.00-21.00 ☏ 42-0091 ⌨ yksm.com

Anbo area

• **Mori-no-kirameki**（森の きらめき）Buy and rent a wide variety of mountain gear. You can also register your mountain trip here. ⏲ 07.30-19.00 ☏ 49-7101 ⌨ morinokirameki.com

THE PORTABLE TOILETS

One of the solutions that had been successfully tried to combat increasing numbers of hikers and the pollution that this can cause are the portable toilets.

Portable toilet cabin interior

These wooden cabins contain only a seat to which you are supposed to attach a portable toilet kit which covers the seat and keeps any contents safely sealed until you reach a disposal unit at the trail entrance.

The toilet kit is small enough to fit in any small backpack and can be bought from a variety of places on Yakushima. One costs ¥400 and two, ¥500.

Portable toilet cabin exterior

SAFETY ON THE TRAILS

The paths are generally safe and easy to follow but can be slippery and treacherous sometimes even on the most widely used trails.

Like all mountainous areas, be aware that accidents do happen and fatalities do occur. All the paths should be clearly marked with small pink ribbons tied to trees and the popular routes to Jomon Sugi and Miyanoura have wooden steps and walkways. It is however still possible to get lost especially when the weather deteriorates and care needs to be taken not to mistakenly follow a deer trail.

There are many registered guides offering their services on Yakushima (but mostly in Japanese) and a lot of tourists hire them for their hiking trips into the mountains. There is a regulatory body called the **Yakushima Guide Association**（屋久島ガイド協会）☏ 49-4191 ⌨ yakushima-guide.com and be careful to check that any potential guide is a member of this organisation as all members have adequate training and support. For a guide in English try Cameron at yakushimaexperience.com or ☎ 090-7820-3592.

The benefit of having a guide is local knowledge of the flora and fauna, the trails and some security should there be an accident. For most people, provided they use common sense and have a basic awareness of what hiking in these mountains involves, a guide is not necessary as the trails are well marked and in generally good condition.

Tozan Todoke box

If you hike outside of an organised group it is suggested that you fill in a climbing form called a **'Tozan todoke'** (登山届け). This is a form (in Japanese) in which you are supposed to detail your route and destination. To fill it in simply put your details, the address where you are staying and the dates and destinations of your hike (anywhere on the form in English is fine). This information is in case of an accident and with it the rescuers know where to begin their search. Every year people are rescued but what is not commonly known is that the cost of the rescue operation is passed on and, should

it take days to find you because your route is unknown, it will be your wallet and not only your body that is damaged.

These forms can usually be found at the trail entrance of the main trails where there is usually a wooden box to post your form. They can also be found and handed in at the airport, tourist information, police station, town hall and port. They are also available as a PDF file on yakumonkey.com.

MOUNTAIN RULES

There are few specific mountain rules for hiking in Yakushima - general common sense rules apply e.g. when encountering hikers, those ascending have priority (and etiquette dictates that you are expected to greet each and every hiker who passes). Due to the environmental impact of visitors, a set of hiking rules are promoted by Yakushima authorities.

1. Use the toilets provided.

2. Use the huts for accommodation and only camp in designated areas.

3. Keep to the trail. Follow the pink ribbon markers and be careful not to stray onto deer paths by mistake.

4. If lost, do not descend directly down a valley or follow the path of a river. There are many straight drops and waterfalls which may be hidden by the undergrowth.

5. Do not feed the animals.

6. Do not remove anything from its natural environment.

7. Bring your garbage back with you.

8. Keep the fresh water clean.

If you stay in the huts, this means not washing your cooking equipment in the nearby stream. Everything should be wiped with a damp cloth or tissue and disposed of later off the mountains.

THE MOUNTAIN HUTS

There are a total of 6 mountain huts on Yakushima. All of them offer a dry place to sleep, water from a stream and a toilet but little else, so all equipment for sleeping and cooking have to be carried with you. Depending on the time you visit you could be all alone or there may be a guided group of noisy, snoring tourists.

The huts are at the forefront of the environmental problems faced by the huge numbers of tourists who hike the paths in Yakushima. In high season many of the huts get very busy and it is not uncommon for them to be full, leaving no choice for some but to camp in the restricted area. The toilets also are used beyond their capacity and have begun to pollute the surrounding area. If you stay in the huts be aware of the problems and try not to add to them. Remember, Yakushima is a World Heritage site and wild camping and camp fires are forbidden.

SHIRATANI HUT (白谷山荘小屋)

Sleeps: 40

Material: Reinforced Concrete

Altitude: 825 m

This hut is 2.1 km (1 hour 20 min) from Shiratani Unsuikyo car park which makes it a popular hut to start from. The toilet is actually inside which, especially in summer, can cause odour problems. It has a wooden communal area to prepare food and also has three rooms with wooden slats to sleep on. Like all the huts it is first come, first served and if the rooms are full, find a place in the communal area.

Shiratani hut

YODOGAWA HUT (淀川小屋)

Sleeps: 60

Material: Wood

Altitude: 1380 m

The Yodogawa hut can be reached via Anbo on the Yakusugiland/Kigensugi mountain road.

It is a 45 min hike (1.5 km) from the Yodogawa trail Entrance and because of its close proximity it can be a very popular hut to stay in. In high season it can get crowded with hikers who take the road up in the late afternoon and begin their hiking to Miyanoura dake the following morning.

TAKATSUKA HUT (高塚小屋)

Sleeps: 20

Material: Concrete-blocks

Altitude: 1330 m

This small hut is only a 10 min walk (200 m) from Jomon Sugi and consequently can get very busy. Water is piped and flows nearby. There are split level wooden racks to sleep on and there is a separate toilet hut.

Yodogawa hut interior

SHIN-TAKATSUKA HUT (新高塚小屋)

Sleeps: 60

Material: Concrete/Wood

Altitude: 1460 m

This hut is 1 km further up the trail and is a hike of just over 1 hour from Takatsuka hut. The sleeping is split level with ladders up to the higher wooden platform. There is an open space in front of the hut for cooking, piped fresh water from the river and a separate toilet nearby.

SHIKANOSAWA HUT (鹿之沢小屋)

Sleeps: 20

Building structure: Stone

Altitude: 1550 m

On the Nagata trail 1.2 km from the summit of Nagata dake. The toilet is in a separate hut 50 m down the Nagata trail across the stream where drinking water is available. Sleeping is split level. The Nagata trail is long and arduous, the Hanayama trail is not popular and few people climb Nagata dake after climbing Miyanoura dake so the hut is usually quite empty.

ISHIZUKA HUT (石塚小屋)

Sleeps: 20

Material: Concrete-blocks

Altitude: 1600 m

This is 1.2 km (50 min) down the Ishizuka trail from Hana-no-ego marsh or 7.2 km (6 hours) up on the same trail from Yakusugiland. The toilet hut is a few meters away and water is from a stream 5 min along the path to Hana-no-ego. According to local people the hut is supposed to be haunted with the ghosts of an American bomber crew who crashed near Hana-no-ego marsh during the Second World War.

SHELTERS

As an alternative to the huts if the weather closes in when around the high peaks, there are several cave like rock formations which provide shelter and some of them have plastic sheeting and other equipment stored for emergencies. For example, **Hiraishi Iwaya** (平石岩屋) on the path up to Miyanoura can sleep up to 8 people in an emergency.

Cave shelter on Yodogawa Trail

8 TRAILS

ARAKAWA – OKABU TRAIL

(荒川-大株歩道)

The Arakawa Trail is by far the busiest trail in Yakushima as it leads on to the great Jomon Sugi, the goal of most visitors to Yakushima.

Most hikers depart along the trail early in the morning and in noisy

Hiking

Timing

▲ 5 hours ▼ 4½ hours (10.6 km one way)

Access

CAR: In order to protect the trail and the road that leads to it, private cars are prohibited from driving to the trail entrance. Instead several shuttle buses leave Yakusugi Museum car park and relay hikers to the start of the trail. Taxis and private tours can also drive up to the entrance but only with a pre-bought access ticket for every hiker.

BUS: Buses in early morning and late afternoon (See Bus Timetables at the beack for more details).

The Trail

guided groups. You can avoid these groups for much of the trail if you leave slightly later on but you will inevitably meet them somewhere along the route. Hiking out of season is the only way to avoid this. The Arakawa trail begins at a mountain sub-station of the logging railway which despite appearances is still very much in use. Until you reach the beginning of the Okabu trail (大株歩道), the trail consists solely of walking on these rail road tracks (for a painful 9.1 km). Start by crossing the suspension bridge, go through the short tunnel which illuminates automatically as you pass through and from the rusty old engine on the right it is a 50 min walk (2.6 km) to **Kosugidani village** (小杉谷集落跡). Signs inform you periodically of 'rest' places to shelter from the train and be aware of them as you may have to jump out of the way of rumbling wagons.

Logging railway

Just before Kosugidani the track separates (careful not to continue on the branch straight on) and veers sharply right to **Kosugidani Bridge** (小杉谷橋). Anbo River below ranges from a gentle trickle to a raging torrent and signs of its power lie in the huge boulders

dragged down the mountain dotted along the river bed.

Once you have crossed the bridge, you are in Kosugidani and the rail track turns left continuing on the opposite bank. Be careful however not to miss the remains of this once vibrant logging village. There are displays of the large logging community that once made this place their home until the logging office was closed in 1970. At its height there were around 600 inhabitants, over 100 of them being children. The old elementary school to the right just after you cross the bridge allows you access to the river. It is reputed to be haunted here so take that into account if you linger after dark. There is also a shelter with more displays, a bio-toilet and piped drinking water to fill up any containers you have.

The path follows the old railway track for what will feel like an eternity from now on. It has a slight uphill gradient and meanders around the mountain slopes, crossing two smaller bridges. On the way there are a few landmarks to break up the monotony. The Kusugawa trail leading from Shiratani meets the railway after 1.8 km at **Kusugawa junction** (楠川分かれ) and there is a clearly marked sign informing you of the fork in the trail.

It is tempting on the way back to take this route as you tire of the railroad, but be aware that the trail is uphill for 1 hour from here and quite steep in places.

A short while after this (2 km after Kosugidani) you come across the first of the grand Yakusugis: **Sandaisugi** (三代杉) or 'Third Generation Ceder'. This is so called because when the original cedar fell, which was estimated at 1,200 years old, a second cedar grew on its remains. This then grew to be over 1,000 years old before being cut down by loggers, whereupon a third then perched itself on top and is currently around 350 years old. The tree stands at 38 m and is well worth a stop as you can see clearly how the generations have grown over one another with roots like tentacles grasping the ground.

Just as you start cursing taking this uncomfortably uneven path and after a further 3.7 km of pounding the railway slats, it abruptly ends at the **Okabu Trail Entrance** (大株歩道入口).

Okabu Trail Entrance

OKABU TRAIL (Lower)

There is little more here than a modern toilet building across a short bridge and a sign pointing to raised wooden steps up into the forest. The rest of the path will mercifully be within the forest.

There is a sign in Japanese here and to save you scratching your head wondering whether it says anything important. Here is a short translation of what it informs tired hikers:

• The path becomes steep from here on.

• You should leave this point before 10.00 as it takes 4 hours to make the return trip from here from Jomon Sugi.

• You should leave Jomon Sugi at 13.00 to return to this point in good time especially if you have a health condition or in bad weather.

• You should visit the toilet here as it is the only regular toilet before Jomon Sugi.

• You should not leave any rubbish.

It is a short 30 minute (400 m) slog up from this sign to the remains of **Okina sugi** (翁杉). This was until 2010 a great Yakusugi that stood at 24 m and was thought to be 2,000 years old. The mostly hollow base however could not hold the tree's weight and all but 3 m collapsed.

Depending on the time you come, you may be passing many exhausted hikers already digging into their food supplies but you are only 200 m from another major milestone on the route:

Wilson's Stump (ウィルソン株). Although sounding like a rather nasty medical complaint, it is in fact a tree stump so large (a circumference of 13.8 m) that it contains within it a shrine and a stream.

The tree that stood here is thought to have been cut down 300 years ago and it was not until a British botanist named **Ernest Henry Wilson** (1876-1930) was led to the stump that it was introduced to the rest of the world in 1914 and like many other species he introduced from Asia, bears his name. Because of the numbers of people passing through this way you can no longer get close. There is a sign in Japanese which tells people not to camp in this area, not to go too near to the stump, not to start any fires and generally to be considerate to other hikers. It is a popular place to stop so if you want to experience it quietly see it early morning or late afternoon.

Wilson's Stump

The path then becomes a mixture of wooden platforms and the forest floor as you pass some of the other grand Yakusugi trees. **Daio-sugi** (大王杉) is 1 hour 10 min (1 km) further down the track. It is estimated to be 3,000 years old and it is largely hollow at its base. Shortly after (100 m) you are greeted by a pair of trees called **Meoto-sugi** (夫婦杉). The 'husband' tree is on the right and is thicker in diameter than the 'wife' on the left who in turn is taller. A horizontal branch has grown between them to join the two trunks together hence the coupling of the trees.

There are several piped drinking water springs – watch out for them on the way and keep filling up your water supplies. Again, it will seem like forever but, after only another 30 min (700 m), one of the bends in the path will bring you to a large raised platform in front of which is the holy grail of Yakusugi trees, **Jomon Sugi** (縄文杉).

It depends on whole range of factors as to how impressed you will be by visiting the most famous tree of all. The weather, the time, the amount of people (up to 500 people a day visit the tree), your level of exhaustion, the distance you are from the tree (15 m) – these all make a difference. There are even sometimes singers and boy bands with TV satellite link broadcasts from the tree! Like Wilson's Stump, if you want the tree all to yourself, late afternoon and early morning are better.

Hikers are restricted to the platform due to the damage done by the ever increasing numbers of tourists. Remember the tree is a national treasure so do not attempt to get any closer to it. Souvenir-hunting tourists scraped a piece of bark (10 x 10 cm) from the tree in 2005 which made national news and required experts from all over Japan to ensure the tree's survival. There is also a recently constructed fence to prevent the deer from grazing on newly planted saplings.

A covered shelter is just around the bend after Jomon sugi and then it is a short 10 min hike (200 m) to the **Takatsuka hut** (高塚小屋) and fresh drinking water. For obvious reasons this hut is popular and can fill up quickly in high season so a second larger hut was built an hour (1 km) up the path called the **Shin-Takatsuka hut** (新高塚小屋). If you are continuing up to Miyanoura dake this may be a better choice.

It is important not under-estimate the Arakawa path up to Jomon Sugi. It is not a gentle wander through the forest but places you high in the central mountains (Jomon Sugi is at 1280 m) and walking a distance of 10.6 km one way in sometimes difficult terrain. It is necessary to be prepared with proper equipment and supplies (see the hiking equipment section) and the trail can also sometimes be slippery and potentially dangerous with many of the bridges holding little or no protection from falling.

Despite the potential dangers, hikers of all ages manage to successfully complete this trail, including children, and with good preparation it is a reasonable day trip.

Overall, the path can be incredibly monotonous in places, especially the railroad, and in comparison with some of the other trees on the island which are less visited and more accessible (yet equally impressive), Jomon Sugi can be a letdown. But as there are no sweeping views on the path, if it is cloudy and raining, despite the soggy waterproofs, it is still perfectly fine to hike.

In fact, try not be too disheartened if the weather closes in, the forest can often be just as beautiful in the rain. And unless you are particularly interested in the local flora and fauna or have health and safety concerns, a guide is not necessary as the path is clearly marked all the way. Try to see it very early or very late in the day before or after the tour groups spoil the peace with their chatter and bright raincoats.

YODOGAWA TRAIL

(淀川歩道)

Hiking

Timing

• To Kuroimi dake: ▲ 3½ hours ▼ 2½ hours (5.3 km one way)

• To Miyanoura dake: ▲ 5 hours ▼ 4 hours (7.8 km one way)

Access

CAR: The road after Yakusugiland winds up, twisting and turning its way to **Kigen sugi** (紀元杉) which stands beside the road, accessible by wooden steps. From then on the road is narrow until the small car park and toilet block at the end which is often full by day-break. If so, park at the nearest safe place on the main road. It should take 30 min by car from Yakusugiland.

BUS: Take the bus to Kigen sugi (紀元杉) and continue on the road or alternatively go on foot from Yakusugiland for 8 km (2½ hours).

The Trail

The Yodogawa trail entrance (淀川登山口) begins with wooden steps up into the forest.

Yodogawa Trail Entrance

It then alternates with wooden steps or platforms and the forest floor for much of the 1.5 km (45 min) to the **Yodogawa hut** (淀川小屋). There is fresh water in the stream behind – go through the gap in the trees to the left of the hut.

There is a toilet across the path from the hut and flat land to cook or eat on. It is usually very popular and can get busy at the end of the day.

Once you cross the river the path is relentlessly uphill, zigzagging its way upwards. Occasionally it

becomes very steep and there are ropes to help you clamber up the rocks, but nothing overly risky, even for children.

After around 90 min the path will level out and through the gaps in the trees you will begin to glimpse a strange curiosity at the top of one of the lower peaks. This is **Koban dake** (高盤岳) and famously looks like chopped tofu. It marks the fact that you are now at **Hana-no-ego marsh** (花之江河), the southern-most highland natural marsh in Japan.

Hana-no-ego marsh is a wetland of international importance and home to Tago's brown frog (ヤクシマタゴガエル), a native subspecies and they can be seen lurking just below the water. It is also the only known home to a freshwater shellfish, 'Pisidium habei' (ハベマメシジミ). It is a common sight to see deer grazing around as you walk on the raised planks and you can stop at the occasional viewing platform.

Hana-no-eigo marsh

There are three other trails that lead off from the marsh. To the left is the **Yudomari trail** (湯泊歩道) / **Kurio trail** (栗生歩道) which both lead all the way down to the coast. To the right is the 50 min trail to the **Ishizuka hut** (石塚小屋) and on from that a further 7 km to **Yakusugiland**. The central mountains are all located on the main trail which bends to the left and to the right but is essentially straight on.

It is now just a short way (25 min) to the junction for **Kuromi dake** (黒味岳) at 1831 m. It comes after a large rock and is signposted to the left. This detour takes you via ropes and some scrambling (30 min) to the top of Kuromi dake and gives you sweeping 360° views. It is a good spot for photos of Miyanoura dake and for surveying the path that leads ahead above the tree line. For those who have had enough of trekking at this point, this is a popular destination in itself.

Kuromi dake

Soon after the turn off to Kuromi the path brings you above the tree line. If the weather is clear, there should be beautiful views as you follow the trail upwards.

Keep slogging on (still three km to go) and you end up ascending as much as you are descending as the path cuts a fairly straight line at various proximities to the ridgeline of the summits of **Nageishi dake** (投石岳) 1830 m, **Anbo dake** (安房岳)

1847 m, **Okina dake** (翁岳) 1860 m, and **Kurio dake** (栗生岳) 1867 m. At this height, the trees have given way to grassland and most of it is small evergreen bamboo grass, native to Yakushima, and known as 'dwarf bamboo'. There are also Yakushima Rhododendrons which bloom in late spring/early summer and an officially organised hike called 'Shakunage Tozan' marks the beginning of their blooming season.

As you continue on the trail, the landscape gradually becomes more barren and the presence of many windswept Yakusugi skeleton trees give it an altogether different feel to the forest below you.

The final climb up to the peak of **Miyanoua dake** (宮之浦岳) at 1935 m is a steep one. There are a number of small caves and a shrine on the way in which you can shelter should the weather take a turn for the worse. When you do finally reach the top there are enough rocks to break the wind but no covered shelter. On a clear day the views of the whole island and beyond are spectacular.

Miyanoura dake

OKABU TRAIL （大株歩道）

(Higher)

Hiking

Timing

Miyanoura dake – Jomon Sugi: ▲ 5½ hours ▼ 4 hours (5.3 km one way)

Miyanoura dake – Nagata dake: ▲ 1 hour ▼ 50 mins (2.5 km one way)

The Trail

Some hikers then continue on either to **Nagata dake** （永田岳） which stands at 1886 m with the option of staying at the **Shikanosawa hut** （鹿之沢小屋） or descend to the **Shin-Takatsuka hut** （新高塚小屋） towards Jomon Sugi.

If you continue on, it is a steep climb down initially and then a more gentle gradient. The junction of the trails, **Yakino-sansaro** （焼野三叉路）, is only a 15 minute walk. The ascent of Nagata dake from Miyanoura dake is not as easy as the 1.5 km distance might appear. The path is often overgrown and you need to descend and then re-

ascend all over again in the short distance between the two peaks.

In all it should take around 50 min from the junction to the summit. On a clear day you can look down on Nagata village and far into the East China Sea and to your right is **Shojidake** （障子岳）, a distinctive wall-like mountain that drops into the valley. Especially in summer be careful of over exposure to the sun as there is little shade at this altitude. Also if you are returning to the Yodogawa entrance be prepared with a flashlight just in case it takes longer than you had planned.

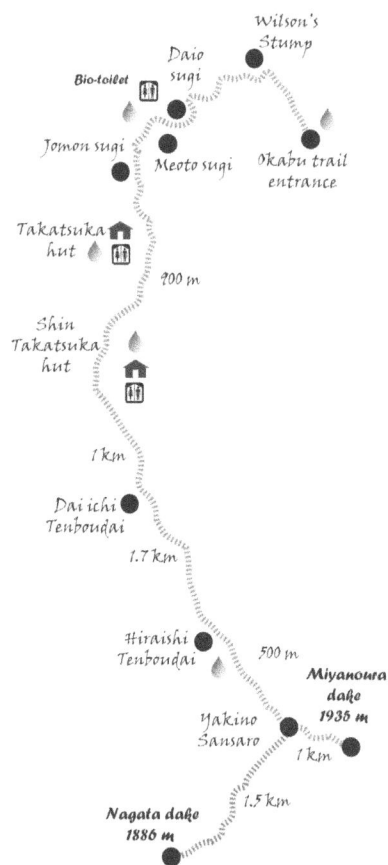

If you are staying in the Shikanosawa hut, there is still a way to go from the summit of Nagata dake, so give yourself enough time to cover the 1.2 km (around 70 min).

It is easy to reach the summit and believe that you have arrived at your destination only to be in despair when you have to walk for another hour. If however you are continuing the descent on towards Jomon sugi, from the junction it is 30 min before you pass **Hiraishi Tenboudai** (平石展望台), a lookout point with wonderful views and a stream for water. Then just over an hour before you cover the 1.7 km to **Dai-ichi Tenboudai** (第一展望台) and the **Shin-Takatsuka hut**, with water and shelter, is a 50 min downward hike from there.

Kusugawa Trail

KUSUGAWA TRAIL
(楠川歩道) (Lower)

Hiking

Timing

▲ 1½ hours ▼ 1 hours (2 km one way) to Shiratani Unsuikyo

Access

CAR: The road is signed towards the mountain from the main road in Kusugawa. Follow the single lane road to the end where there is a sign for the Kusugawa Mountain Trail Entrance (楠川登山道入口). There is no real car park as such but park your car at the side where the road ends.

BUS: Get off at No.37 Kusugawa (楠川) bus stop, a few kilometres south from Miyanoura. The trail is clearly signed on the mountain side of the main road and it is a 1 hour walk to the trail entrance (3.2 km).

The Trail

Kusugawa trail begins near the coast and is a useful hiking alternative to taking the mountain road up to **Shiratani Unsuikyo**.

Kusugawa

Kusugawa Trail
Entrance

1.6 km

Shiratani
Unsuikyo

from a bygone age when logging was still the main industry on Yakushima.

There are rarely more than a handful of hikers who take this trail and there are often macaques and deer foraging nearby.

Macaques on Kusugawa Trail

Pink ribbons mark the trail upwards and it is quite steep but eventually (after 1½ hours) you should reach a gravel road.

Trail junction at Shiratani Unsuikyo

The trail is initially paved from the trail entrance but soon you reach the canopy of the forest and underfoot is nothing but the dirt of the forest floor. Occasionally logging takes place in this area so there may be machinery or signs of tree cutting dotted around.

It is a relatively simple trail to follow as it was part of the main Edo Period (1603-1868) logging path and along the way you will come across the brick remains of charcoal ovens and other leftovers

Turn right onto the road and you have a choice of going straight ahead to the entrance of Shiratani Unsuikyo (with toilets and buses) or follow the marked path to your left which is a continuation of the Kusugawa trail and which joins the Shiratani paths a short while further on.

SHIRATANI UNSUIKYO

（白谷雲水峡）

Hiking

Timing

From 1 hour to 5 hours (depending on your choice of trail)

Access

CAR: The mountain road is clearly sign posted (in English) from Route 77 in Miyanoura. Route 594 meanders up for 12 km, climbs 800 m and takes around 30 min by car. The road has been improved over the past few years but there are still some tight spots higher up where it is still single track. The free car park is past the entrance hut and over the bridge, although if it is full you have to park on the main road leading up to the park.

BUS: There are several buses a day from Miyanoura. Check the bus timetables at the back of the book.

The Trails

Shiratani Unsuikyo centres on a tributary of Miyanoura river and covers over 420 hectares of evergreen broad leaf forest. The entrance is at 620 m and consists of a collection of wooden huts which mark the beginning of the trail. If you enter here you have to pay ¥300 (but not if you keep to the Kusugawa trail). The toilets are across the bridge on the way from the main car park.

A large map stands at the entrance of Shiratani. It details the routes of several colour-coded courses to follow. If you come via the main entrance and pay the entrance fee, you are given a map (it is available in English) of all the routes. The Yayoi sugi Cedar course is 60 min and can be done in normal footwear, but the Kusugawa hiking course (1 hour 40 min), the Primeval forest course (3 hours) and the Taikoiwa rock trail (5 hours) all require proper mountain shoes and basic equipment like waterproofs, a backpack, food and a container for water. (See the hiking equipment section for more details).

The path follows the river for the first section of steps and walkways. After a short while there will be a fork to the right to **Yayoi sugi** cedar tree (弥生杉) - this is worth the 500 m detour as it is one of the oldest Yakusugi at 3,000 years of age. The path consists of platforms and stone steps and although you can no longer touch it, you can get close enough. Late afternoon or early morning you should have the tree all to yourself.

If you take the path to Yayoi sugi you can continue on the trail and after 600 m you will rejoin the main path further up. If you do this you avoid a giant rock called **Oiwa rest place** (憩いの大岩) on the main path where the wooden steps give way to climbing up the rock face

Taikoiwa
rock

↑ Okabu Trail

Tsuji toge
pass

Nanahonsugi

Shiratani
hut

Kugurisugi

Nidai-kugurisugi

Primeval forest
trail

Sanbon-
yarisugi

Caution
after heavy
rain

Kusugawa
trail

Buqyosugi

Bibinkosugi

Sanbon-ahisugi

Satsuki-
tsurihashi
bridge

Nidai-osugi

Yayoi
trail

Yayoisugi

Entrance

Kusugawa
trail

Miyanoura
by road

→

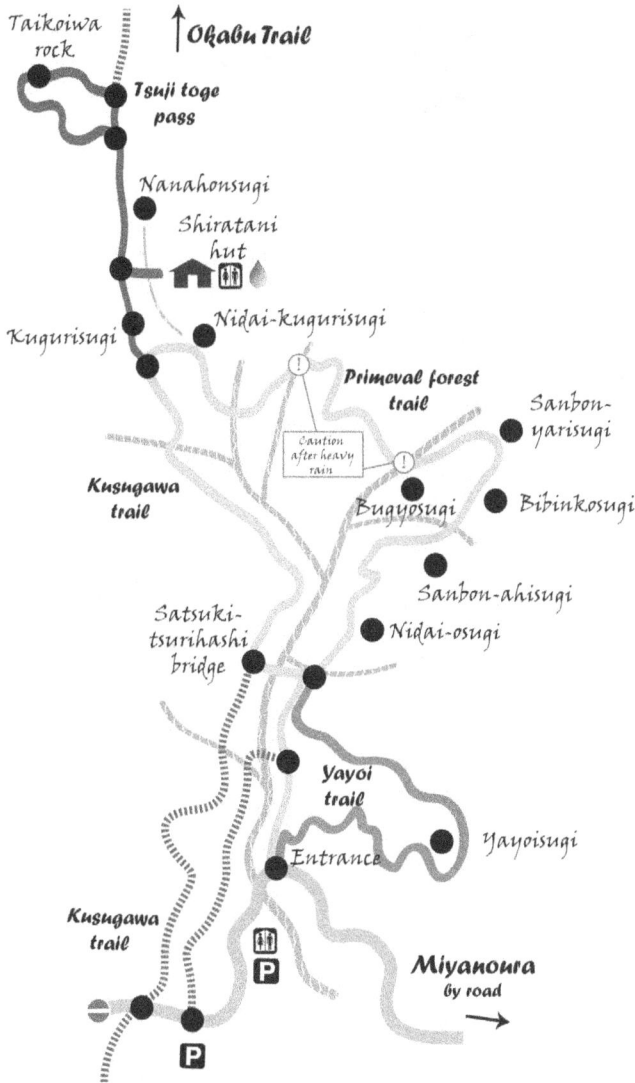

for a few metres. The wooden steps begin again soon after and when both paths have met again, the main attraction in this part of Shiratani is the waterfall which runs to the side of the trail called **Hiryu Otoshi** (飛流おとし). In rainy season the water gushes down, but at other times you can get closer and follow stone steps on to the rocks. If you keep climbing, you come to the end of the tree covered path where the **Satsuki-tsuribashi** (さつき吊橋) suspension bridge crosses the valley.

Oiwa rest place

Cross the bridge and you will come to an extension of the **Kusugawa trail** (楠川歩道) that began down at the coast (See the Kusugawa Trail for more details) and which continues up to **Shiratani hut** (白谷山荘) and beyond. The path was laid in the Edo period and is fairly straight and solid. You have to cross one river on stepping stones so proceed with caution after rain. Stay on the same side of the river and continue straight ahead, however, for a meandering hike through pristine damp forest with uneven trails and rivers to hop over.

Primeval Hiking trail

This is the **Genseirin (Primeval Forest) Hiking trail** (原生林歩道). Again be cautious after rain as the river levels can make the trail hazardous. The forest here is as you might see in magazines and postcards about Yakushima and it includes several important yakusugi trees.

In the end both trails end in the same place, at the foot of the short path to Shiratani hut, and if you wanted to go no further up the mountain, this trail can be a worthwhile circular trip, returning on the Kusugawa trail.

Around 200 m along the trail is the second of the grand cedars, **Nidai-Osugi** (二代大杉). It stands above a small stream and at 32 m, is one of the tallest Yakusugi in Shiratani. '二代' means 'second generation' and the tree is the product of germination on top of a fallen cedar. Over the years the original tree decayed and the gap is left where that tree once stood.

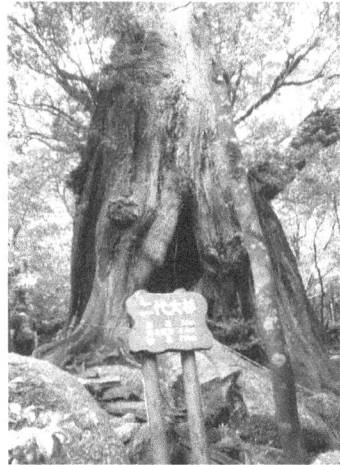

Nidai-Osugi

The trail then snakes its way up for the next 500 m to **Sanbonashi-sugi** (三本足杉) which stands like a tripod on the forest floor. Its strange shape is due to the same process as that of Nidai-Ohsugi. The host tree fell, the second generation cedar grew over it and when the host tree decayed and withered away, the open space remained.

You soon have to cross a bridgeless river and care must be taken especially after heavy rain. You have to jump from rock to rock but keep an eye out for the pink ribbons to keep on the trail.

Sanbonashi-sugi

The next cedar, **Bibinkosugi** (びびん こ杉), is 100 m further on. This is a young cedar at just 350 years old and its name was chosen in 1999 by a local junior high school teacher, Takeshi Wakita (脇田武志). 'びびんこ' means 'piggy-back' (肩車) in Kagoshima dialect and was chosen to reflect the second generation growth so common in the cedar trees in Yakushima.

The path then makes a gradual turn towards **Sanbonyari-sugi** (三本 槍杉) which means '3 spears cedar' and its name becomes clear when you see that three trees appear to stem from one slanted trunk. The host tree is thought to be around 800 years old but two of the 'spears' are second generation cedars, the third is actually thought to be one of the original branches.

Continue on and **Bugyosugi** (奉行 杉) lies across another river. There was an attempt to cut down the tree in the Edo period borne out by the marks on the trunk. Bugyo '奉行 ' means 'Magistrate', named so because it is believed that the local

Magistrate took a rest beside the tree while visiting the forest. It is not particularly tall at 24 m but it makes up for this in trunk thickness with a circumference of 8.5 m.

Nidai-Kugurisugi (二代くぐり杉) is soon before the branch of the trail that leads up towards Shiratani hut and you will find yourself walking through its trunk.

You have the choice here of continuing on the same trail which will bring you back to Shiratani entrance or take the trail upwards through the two giant legs of **Kugurisugi** (くぐり杉) before the ground levels off and **Shiratani hut** (白谷山荘) is signed to your right.

At Shirtatani hut there is a river for drinking water, shelter if you need it and a not too pleasant smelling toilet within. There is a large communal area inside and there are a few separate rooms to sleep in. Outside there are some large tables and benches to sit on. It is a popular place for deer and they can often be spotted munching away amongst the trees.

Shiratani Hut

The main destination after Shiratani hut is **Taikoiwa Rock** (太鼓 岩), a 30 minute hike further up the mountain. The trail becomes steeper and rocky as it rises but the forest opens out and there is more a feeling of space.

Soon you will pass **Nanahonsugi** (七本杉), a cedar so named because of its seven branches, although two have dropped off over the years now leaving only five. You will then come across what was temporarily known as Mononoke forest, named because of the local connection with the Ghibli studios' animated movie 'Princess Mononoke' (もののけ姫). It has since been renamed due to copyright but anyway, this is more a creation for tired, hurried tourists who need a goal to walk to rather than a particularly beautiful piece of forest. If you took the 150 minute course to get there you would have seen far more beautiful sights.

When you reach the top of the trail, the 979 m high point of **Tsujitoge pass** (辻峠), there are some wooden benches and signs in Japanese. Taikowa rock (太鼓岩) is to the left with two short paths and the Tsujitoge pass continues straight on. To climb up to Taikoiwa rock you are supposed to

ascend on the path furthest from you and return on the one nearest. You may get some grumbling from stumbling hikers and their guides if you choose the wrong one. The trees are tightly packed and the going is very hard but it is only a short distance (15 min) before you reach the gap in the undergrowth and you are breathtakingly surveying the whole of the central mountain range with Anbo River gushing in the distance.

If you choose to continue further on the path, it descends rapidly to join the forest railroad and the Arakawa trail after 50 min (1.4 km). You will pass **Tsuji grotto** (辻の岩屋) which is the gap created between a horizontal laying giant boulder and the rocks it rests on. It can fit 5-6 people underneath and is used as an emergency mountain shelter. This route from Shiratani over Tsujitoge pass is often used as an alternative to the Arakawa trail and the Okabu hiking trail to Jomon Sugi and Miyanoura dake. It is especially useful when the road to Arakawa Trail Entrance is blocked.

YAKUSUGILAND

（やくすぎランド）

Hiking

Timing

From ½ hour to 2½ hours (depending on your choice of trail)

Access

CAR: Yakusugiland can be reached from the main mountain road from Anbo. The road snakes up the mountains for 16 km and has been widened and improved in places over the past few years. There is a car park at the entrance with attendants in high season to direct you to a parking place.

BUS: There are regular buses (check the bus timetables)

The Trails

The car park is opposite a large wooden building to the left, the Shizen (森泉) Resthouse, which has a small souvenir shop and toilets in it. The entrance (¥300 for adults) to the park is opposite this building and a giant map displays the various courses according to how long they take to complete.

30 MIN COURSE ↻

This path is paved or on wooden walkways and can be followed with any footwear. It is popular with less able tourists who want to get the briefest of tastes of the forest.

➲ **Entrance** (入口)

➲ **Kuguritsuga** (くぐり栂) is a hemlock spruce not a cedar tree. It is around 300 years old and stretches across the stone path like an entrance gate. It is so named because the verb 'くぐる' means

Hana-no-ego & Ishizuka hut

Mitsunesugi
Hahakosugi
Tachu dake 1497 m

Sawatsubashi bridge
Tenchusugi
Tenmon forest

Tenchubashi bridge
Jamonsugi
Bio-toilet

Kokenohashi bridge
Higechoro

Kobana trail

Buddasugi
Arakawabashi bridge

Sennensugi

Futagosugi
Kuguritsuga

Entrance
Anbo

Kugurisugi
Shizen Resthouse

Risenbashi bridge

Exit

Seiryobashi bridge

Kigensugi

'to go under'.

⮑ **Rinsenkyo Bridge** (林泉橋) is the first of the suspension bridges in Yakusugiland that span a tributary of Anbo River, the Arakawa.

⮑ **Sennensugi hiking trail** (千年杉歩道) then takes you to a side path to **Sennensugi** (千年杉) down a series of steps. Sennen '千年' means '1,000 years'

⮑ **Futagosugi** (双子杉) Futago '双子' means 'twins' and two separate cedar trees have grown from the trunk of a felled tree

⮑ **Kugurisugi** (くぐり杉) is similar to Kuguritsuga at the beginning of the path in that the trail goes beneath its upturned V- shaped trunk

⮑ **Seiryo bridge** (清涼橋)

⮑ **Exit** (出口)

50 MIN COURSE ↻

This path brings you closer to the river and further into the forest but has stone or wooden walkways the whole way and can be followed with normal footwear.

⮑ As the 30 min course until Sennensugi hiking trail (千年杉歩道)

⮑ Arakawa hiking trail (荒川歩道)

⮑ **Buddhasugi** (仏陀杉) – this yakusugi cedar is named due the visual resemblance to the face of Buddha on the lower right trunk and estimated to be 1,800 years old

⮑ Buddhasugi hiking trail (仏陀杉歩道)

⮑ Futagosugi (双子杉) then follow the 30 min course.

80 MIN COURSE ↻

A more comprehensive tour of the yakusugi trees, this path is on uneven forest floor and requires shoes fit to hike in.

⮑ As the 50 min course until **Arakawa hiking trail** (荒川歩道)

⮑ **Arakawa bridge** (荒川橋)

⮑ **Tachu junction** (太忠分れ) is the turn off from the trail to the right for the 150 min course and Tachu dake Mountain. Soon after the path comes close to the river and this is a perfect spot for a break on the large rocks spanning across the water.

⮑ **Kokeno Bridge** (苔の橋) means 'moss' bridge and has a shelter with a bench on the opposite side

⮑ **Tsutsujigawara** (つつじ河原) is a lookout point with a small round shelter

⮑ **Sawatsu Bridge** (沢津橋) crosses Arakawa River again

⮑ **Buddhasugi** (仏陀杉) then follow the 50 min course.

150 MIN COURSE ↯

This course leads you much deeper through the forest.

⮑ As the 80 min course until **Tachu junction** (太忠分れ)

⮑ **Kohana hiking trail** (小花歩道) which passes through the 'giant tree' forest of **Kobannayama** (小花山).

Wooden walkway in Yakusugiland

➲ **Higechoro-sugi** (ひげ長老) was named by a local Elementary school student (who won the official naming competition) because the moss at the bottom of the tree resembled an old man's beard

➲ **Portable Bio-toilet**

➲ **Jamonsugi** (蛇紋杉) is near the rest hut at the trail junction. This giant cedar tree was blown down in Sept 1997 by Typhoon No.19 and the tangle of roots weave outwards like a sculpture

➲ **Tenchu Bridge** (天柱橋) used to be made from cedar wood but was washed away in a typhoon

➲ **Tenchusugi** (天柱杉) is 1,500 years old and at 33.8m is one of the tallest yakusugi in Yakushima

➲ **Hahakosugi** (母子杉) -'母' means mother and '子' child and these two cedar trees are so named because they have grown so close to each other. Both are around 2,600 years old. The mother is 31.1m tall (but has already died) and the child slightly shorter at 29 m

➲ **Mitsunesugi** (三根杉) is the thickest of all the yakusugi in Yakusugiland with a diameter of 9.3 m but it is one of the youngest at a sprightly 1,100 years old.

➲ **Sawatsu bridge** (沢津橋) then follow the 80 min course.

There are also 2 mountain trails which begin at Yakusugiland:

TACHU DAKE TRAIL

(太忠岳)

Hiking

Access

Take the 150 minute hiking course in Yakusugiland and when you cross the Arakawa Bridge take the **Kohana hiking trail** for around 500 m to the shelter. Here the path turns sharply left and the trail to Tachu dake is signed straight on and upwards.

The Trail

The mistake that many people make is to under-estimate the Tachu dake trail. It rises up to 1497 m and consists of very steep and rough terrain including ropes and ladders. It is easy to just continue on believing it to be an extension of the Yakusugiland path but be warned, you need lots of time and energy for it to be an enjoyable experience and not a hard slog.

The trail is clearly marked all the way but is very steep in places and sometimes requires scrambling on all fours. Water is available in two streams that run after the rest area of **Tenmon forest** (天文の森) where there is a sign and benches. It then climbs up to a giant boulder which the path skirts around and continues up.

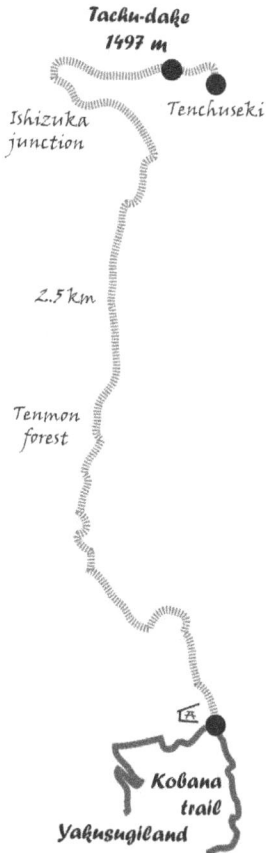

Tachu-dake
1497 m

Ishizuka junction

Tenchuseki

2.5 km

Tenmon forest

Kobana trail

Yakusugiland

The trail then rises very steeply on the way to **Ishizuka junction** (石塚 分かれ) where the path veers left

but then makes a sharp right turn. There is an overgrown trail from this point to the nearby mountain of Hanaoredake (花折岳) but with no public access.

The trail is then a matter of climbing up ladders and ropes until you see the rocks at the summit. It can be confusing when you reach the summit as the path drops down to the side of the bare rock. There is however a rope with which you can pull yourself up to the huge horizontal stone that points out eastwards to Anbo and the sea in the distance. The large rock behind it that points up to the sky is known as **Tenchuseki** (天柱石).

The view from here is well worth the climb and is nothing short of spectacular on a clear day.

The summit of Tachu dake

ISHIZUKA TRAIL

（石塚歩道）

Ishizuka Hut

Hiking

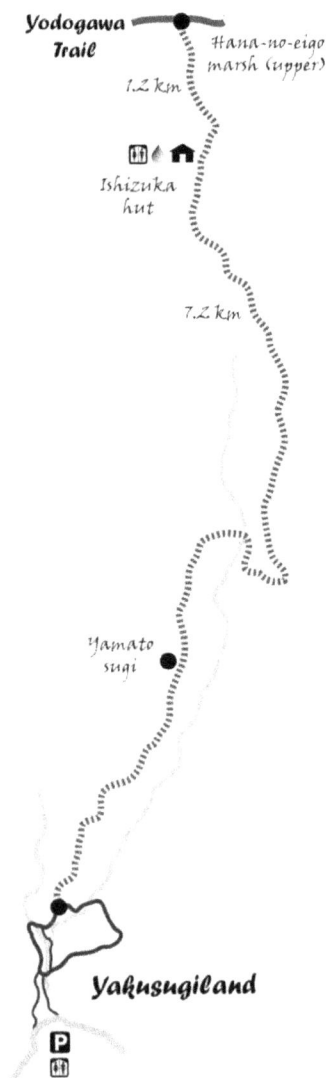

Timing

▲ 6+ hours ▼ 5+ hours (7.2 km to Ishizuka hut /8.4 km to Hana-no-ego)

Access

Take the 150 min hiking course in Yakusugiland and 300 m after **Tenchu Bridge** （天柱橋）there is a sign to **Hana-no-ego marsh** （花之江河）to the right (see Yakusugiland map).

The Trail

From here to the **Ishizuka hut** is a 6 hour slog up an underused path and through several unbridged rivers.

On the way (after around 2 hours) you will come across **Yamato sugi** （大和杉）on your left, a grand yakusugi tree which stands at around 35 m and is estimated to be 3-4,000 years old. From the hut it is a further 45 min before you reach Hana-no-ego marsh.

AIKO DAKE TRAIL

(愛子岳)

Hiking

Timing

▲ 3½ hours ▼ 3 hours (4.4 km one way)

Access

CAR: Signed on Route 77 at the south end of Koseda village. Turn inland and follow the narrow road through gradually thicker forest until you come across the Aiko dake Trail Entrance sign (愛子岳登山口). It is about a 10 min drive. There is a small parking area to the right just before.

BUS: Get off at No.43 Nishi Koseda (西小瀬田) bus stop on the main coastal road and walk past the convenience store. Turn inland at the sign and walk 2.6 km to the trail entrance.

The Trail

The attraction of scaling Aiko dake is that almost the whole path is within the **World Natural Heritage Area protection zone**. It is also,

however, one of the toughest day hikes on the island.

From the outset, you ascend through thick forest and relentlessly climb for two hours until just over 1,000 m. Every few hundred meters there are height markers to inform you of the altitude and once at the highest point a short descent then lulls you into thinking you are almost there but then you have to clamber on your hands and knees over the last even steeper rocky ascent.

There is a small drinkable stream about ½ an hour after the trail veers right (it does this at 984 m).

Aiko dake from a distance

The summit (1235 m) has a series of ropes to pull yourself up a fairly steep rock face and once there you are rewarded with magnificent views of the coast and of the higher inland mountains.

Due to the exposed nature of the summit, it is probably best to avoid it on gusty days.

MOCHOMU DAKE
TRAIL (モッチョム岳)

Hiking

Timing

▲ 3½ hours ▼ 3½ hours (3 km one way)

Access

CAR: Follow the signs to **Senpiro-no-taki waterfall** (千尋の滝) at **Hara** (原). There are several routes from the main road all leading to the same windy 3 km road. Midway it makes a tight right turn but continue until you reach the car park and souvenir store. The trail entrance is on the path to the waterfall viewing area.

BUS: Get off at any one of 3 bus stops in or near Hara. Either get off at No.87 **Tainokawa** (鯛ノ川) bus stop and walk 300 m across the bridge to the signed right turn; Or get off at No.88 **Hara Iriguchi** (原入口) and walk (Onoaida direction) until the park where you turn right; Or get off at No.89 **Hara** (原) and walk (Anbo direction) to the park where you turn left. Whichever stop you get off at it is 3 km (50 min) to the waterfall (and trail entrance).

The Trail

Another very tough hike is to scale the lump of rock that hangs over Onoaida called Mochomu Dake (944 m). The trail begins at the short paved road from the car park to the viewing place at **Senpiro-no-taki waterfall**.

Midway along there is a sign to the left and a trail into the trees. The climb is very steep initially but levels off and then is intermittently steep, often requiring scrambling up on all fours.

After 1½ hours you reach the first of two notable trees, **Bandai sugi** (万代杉), estimated to be 3,000 years old. While its trunk is a solid 8.6 m thickness, it stands at a modest height of only 13 m probably due to exposure to the strong coastal winds. If you look closely it shows evidence of Edo period logging. This is followed by the much taller **Mochomu taro** (モッチョム太郎) which reaches 24 m in height; it too has the scars of loggers.

Once you reach **Kamiyama tembodai** (神山展望台), a viewpoint at the highest point of the trail, an hour later, you then actually start descending for the last 500 m to the summit of Mochomu dake.

The path is usually very quiet and it can be slightly overgrown outside of summer but is easy to follow and there are spectacular views from the top on a clear day.

Mochomu Trail Entrance

ONOAIDA TRAIL

(尾之間歩道)

Access

CAR: Follow signs for Onoaida Onsen (尾之間温泉). At the traffic signals at the far end of Onoaida bypass turn inland and the onsen is at the end of the narrow road. You can park in the car park to the left of the Onsen.

BUS: Get off at No.98 Onoaida Onsen Iriguchi (尾之間温泉入口) bus stop and it is a 20 min walk inland from the traffic signals to the Onsen and the trail head.

Janokuchi waterfall

The Trail

There are two parts to this trail depending on how far you wish to walk. Most hikers take the trail as far as Janokuchi waterfall and then return but the main trail continues high up into the central mountain

range and can be the start of a much longer trip.

⮌ JANOKUCHI WATERFALL (蛇ノ口滝)

Hiking

Timing

▲ 2 hours ▼ ½ hours (3.5 km one way)

If the weather prevents hiking in the central mountains, this trail is a fine alternative. It begins to the right of Onoaida onsen and gently meanders through the forest for an hour before becoming more challenging the closer you come to the waterfall. After 1½ hours (3½ km) the path splits at **Janokuchi-taki junction** (蛇ノ口滝分かれ) and then it is a 20 min hike on the branch path to the waterfall. Because of the river crossings care should be taken after heavy rain.

⮌ YODOGAWA TRAIL ENTRANCE (淀川登山口)

Hiking

Timing

▲ 5½ hours (7½ hours from Onsen) ▼ 4½ hours (5½ hours to Onsen) (8.5 km one way)

Back at **Janokuchi junction** (蛇ノ口滝 分かれ), the main trail continues onwards and steeply upwards.

It takes a further 3 hours (4.5 km) to reach **Tainokawa** (鯛之川) river. You need to cross the river here and do so with caution as after heavy rain it can be untraversable. In 2003 a guide took a group of 5 hikers across Tainokawa and a flash flood washed 3 of them away to their deaths. It is then another 2½ hours (4 km) to the **Yodogawa Trail entrance** (淀川登山口).

RYUJINSUGI TRAIL

(龍神杉登山道)

Hiking

Timing

▲ 4 hours ▼ 3½ hours (5.3 km one way)

Access

CAR: From **Miyanoura Recreational Park** (屋久島総合自然公園) take the small road next to and on the same side of the river (神之川林道). After 3 km there is a left turn (龍神杉登山口) and a very steep hill. This hill will lead you the one km to the trail head (歩道入口). The road is unpaved and will be bumpy without a 4WD. It is possible to park near the trail (limited spaces) although sometimes there are obstructions in the road or you can park back in the car park of Miyanoura Recreational Park and walk one hour to the trail head.

BUS: Get off at No.31 Miyanoura Sho (宮之浦小) bus stop and take the mountain road towards Shiratani Unsuikyo. After crossing a river the road steeply rises and bends to the right. Turn right at the sign for Miyanoura Recreational Park and when you reach the car park at the end (30 min), continue on the unpaved forest road that runs parallel to the river as above.

The Trail

This trail is the old **Yakusando trail** (益救参道) which has been renamed. It is an older path with is not traversed very often and it is more than likely that you will be the only one on it.

For the first hour the trail gently climbs through open forest until at an altitude of around 600 m, the remains of the old logging station (造林小屋跡) leads you on to the disused forest railroad (トロッコ軌道跡). This is from a time when 4 separate forest railroads transported Yakushima's trees

down to the coast but now has a ghostly feel to it with discarded items littering the forest floor.

Follow the railroad track for 20 min and where trees block you from going any further there is a very steep trail to the right. From here onwards, it is relentlessly upwards but the path is clear and not too taxing.

After 1½ hours you cross a river and then a very spooky mountain lodge, **Degoya hut** (出小屋跡), which has collapsed spilling out the belongings of long departed mountain workers. You then cross the same river again but caution is advised here after heavy rain as it can be dangerous. It then becomes steeper again as you climb the last 1 km to the three **Sanjin sugi** (三神杉) trees known individually as Dragon **Ryujin sugi** (龍神杉),

Thunder & Lightning **Raijin sugi** (雷神杉) and Wind **Fujin sugi** (風神杉). There are wooden platforms and steps guiding you on a circular tour of the trees. Go left and as the trail rises, Raijin sugi and Fujin sugi are either side of the trail opposite each other.

There are no signs and few people know which is which but the left tree has the marks of a lightning strike at the rear and perhaps is Raijin sugi. When the trail veers right you have reached the end and there is a platform facing the magnificent Ryujin sugi.

There is a branch of the trail from here which used to lead to Jomon Sugi however the trail is overgrown and no longer used.

NAGATA TRAIL
（永田歩道）

Hiking

Timing

▲ 14 hours to hut/ 16 hours to Nagata dake ▼ 10 hours from hut/ 11½ hours from Nagata dake (12.4 km one way)

Access

CAR: Turn inland just west of Nagata river (永田川) at the gas station. Then take the next left. If you miss it, any one of the roads on the left will take you to the same place. Continue parallel to the river (make sure you do not cross it) and follow the road up for a few minutes. There will be an old weathered sign and a small turning to the left into the Nagata trail car

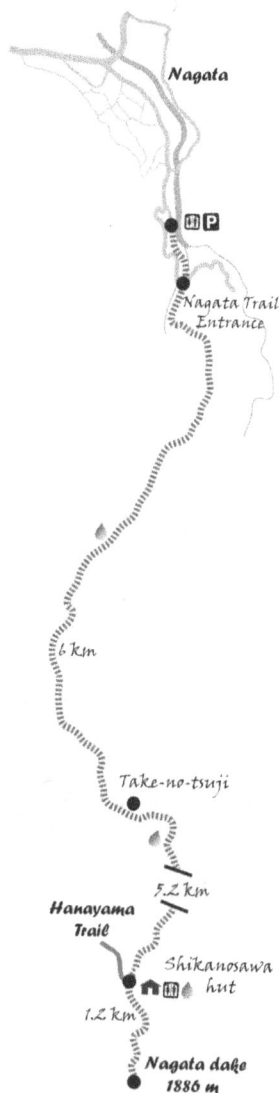

park.

BUS: Get off at No.1 Nagata (永田) bus stop, keep west of the bridge and walk inland. Turn left to keep parallel to the river and walk for 40 min to reach the car park that marks the start of the trail.

The Trail

Nagata Trail is very long (12.4 km) and very tough and should only be attempted if you are prepared for the hard slog. Few but the hardiest venture up to Nagata dake this way.

The Trail Entrance is further on from the car park after you have begun the ascent upwards.

Water is available at 2 places along the way both before and after **Take no Tsuji** (竹の辻) which is the first peak, 6 km into the trail.

Shikanosawa hut (鹿之沢小屋) is waiting at the top for those who do choose this route and after 14 hours of steep climbing, you probably would collapse with exhaustion at the sight of it. As ever the views are spectacular from Nagata dake (永田岳) at 1886 m, which is another 1.2 km or 2 hours up from the hut. But there are of course easier ways to get there! (See the Yodogawa or Okabu trails)

The summit of Nagata dake

KURIO TRAIL (栗生歩道)

Hiking

Timing

Trail entrance to Hana-no-ego: ▲ 4½ hours ▼ 3½ hours (6 km one way)

Access

CAR: Turn inland at the traffic signals before you cross Kurio River and take the Kuromi forest path. A whopping 18½ km later (a 2 hour drive up the rough mountain road) you reach the trail entrance (栗生歩道入口). The only obstacle being that there is a gate to prevent cars going any further than ¾ of the way up.

BUS: Get off at No.127 Kurio-bashi (栗生橋) bus stop and it is a 6½ hour (18.5 km) walk from Kurio to the trail entrance (5½ to return).

The Trail

Once you eventually reach the trail entrance (where there is a small sign to Hana-no-ego) it is a steady upward climb through thick forest to **Logan no tenboudai** (露岩 の 展望台) lookout point for 2½ hours (3.5

km). It is then another 2 hour (3 km) ascent to **Hana-no-ego** marsh (花之江河) at the crossroads of the main mountain paths.

It is a rarely used trail because of the access problems and the sheer distances involved between Kurio and the trail entrance. The trail can however be started much lower

down than the actual trail entrance and begins at an altitude of under 400 m on the Kuromi Forest Path. From here it is a steep but fairly straight climb and enables you to avoid the windy road which snakes over the mountain side.

YUDOMARI TRAIL

(湯泊歩道)

Hiking

Timing

▲ 7 hours ▼ 5 hours (10.5 km one way)

Access

CAR: Take the road inland either side of the village and keep ascending for around 30 min. Eventually there will be a barrier at which point cars are not allowed to cross. The actual start of the trail (湯泊歩道入口) however is considerably further on (two hours).

BUS: Get off the bus at Yudomari (湯泊) bus stop. On foot from Yudomari village to the trail head is around 4 hours (10.5 km).

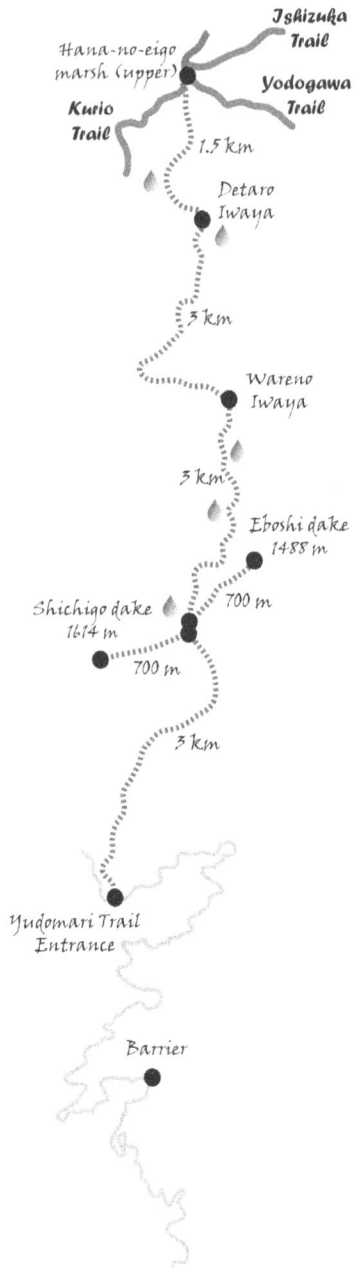

The Trail

Because this path is so rarely used it is not properly signed and can be in a poor state with objects and overgrowth covering the path. There are also many streams to cross. It is therefore potentially hazardous, especially after heavy rain.

The trail has two branch paths in the following order:

• **Shichigo dake** (七五岳)

From the entrance to the turn off for Shichigo dake is a 2 hour (3 km) hike along the trail and the summit of Shichigo dake (1488 m) lay a further 30 min (700 m) climb on a side path.

• **Eboshi dake** (烏帽子岳)

It is only a short walk further on to the second branch on this trail to Eboshi dake (1614 m). The remains of an old hut called **Mino sansha** (ミノ山舎) marks the turn off and there is a stream for water.

The summit of Eboshi dake is a ½ hour (700 m) walk from here. Back at the main path, if you continue to climb for a further 1½ hours (3 km), you will reach **Wareno iwaya** (ワレノ岩屋) which has a very basic grotto for up to 4 people but without water source. There are however 2 streams on the way to collect water. Another 1½ hour (3 km) climb after this and there is another grotto called Detaro iwaya (データロー岩屋). This has enough space for up to 7 people.

There is usually water in the stream nearby but if not 500 m later there is another stream. An hour (1½ km) on from here and the path meets the **Kurio trail** (栗生歩道) as it heads

another ½ an hour upwards to **Hana-no-ego** marsh (花之江河).

HANAYAMA TRAIL
(花山歩道)

Hiking

Timing

▲ 5½ hours ▼ 4½ hours (11 km one way)

Access

CAR: To drive up the Oko forest path you will need a sturdy 4 wheel drive car as the road can be in bad repair in places. It takes around 40 minutes by car to make it to the Hanayama trail entrance (花山歩道入口).

BUS: Get off the bus at No.129 Oko-no-taki waterfall (大川の滝) and walk back for 15 minutes to Oko forest path junction (大川林道分れ). From here it is a 2½ hour walk to the start of the trail.

The Trail

The attraction of this long trail is that it traverses the virgin forests of the protected Yakushima wilderness area. Fill up with water at the trail entrance and it then takes 2½ hours to climb the 3.8 km to Yakimine (焼峰) peak at 1264 m. The trail then levels off for 1 km before rising up a further 1.8 km to Oishitenbodai (大石 展望台) lookout point and beautiful views of the coast. It then continues to climb, crosses Okawa River 3 times and finally reaches Shikanosawa hut (鹿之沢小屋) 1½ hours (2.4 km) on from that.

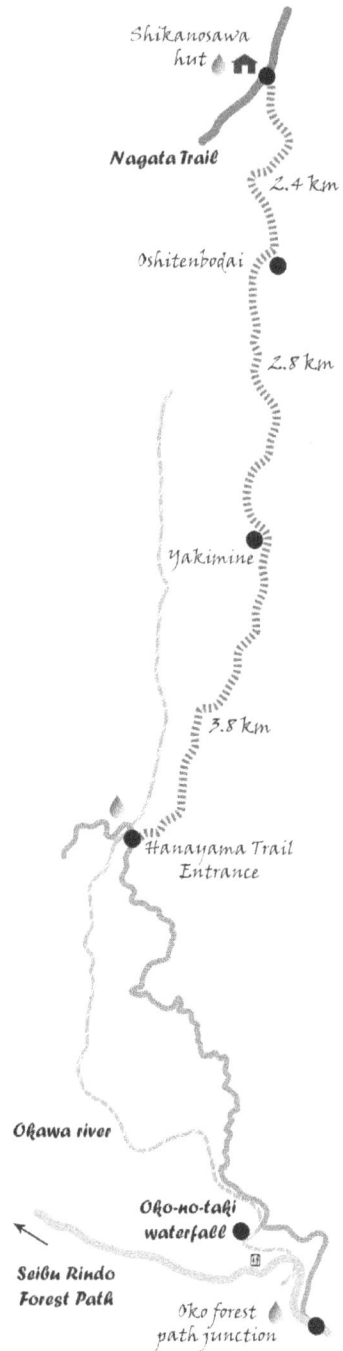

Shikanosawa hut

Nagata Trail

2.4 km

Oshitenbodai

2.8 km

Yakimine

3.8 km

Hanayama Trail Entrance

Okawa river

Oko-no-taki waterfall

Seibu Rindo Forest Path

Oko forest path junction

9 HOT SPRINGS

Yakushima is blessed with several natural hot springs. What better way to finish off a day's hiking with a soak in a hot bath. They range from the deluxe hotel based baths to the free outside natural hot rock pools. So should you get the urge to strip off with a bunch of complete strangers, you will find the following list very helpful.

♨ **Oura Onsen** (大浦の湯) is a 25 min drive from Miyanoura heading towards Nagata and signposted between Yoshida and Isso. Very small and basic next to the beach. ⏱ 11.00 to 19.00 Price: ¥300. ☎ 44-2800

Oura Onsen

♨ **Kusugawa Onsen** (楠川温泉) is signposted towards the mountains on the main road in Kusugawa. It has a small bath and only a handful of people at a time can bathe. Artificially heated. Price: ¥300. ⏱ 09.00 – 20.00. ☎ 42-1166

♨ **Jomon-no-yado Manten** (縄文の宿 まんてん) is opposite the airport in Koseda. Price includes towel, yukata, soap, shampoo and use of the relaxation room with comfy massage chairs. Outdoor/indoor

bath. The water is partly artificially heated. ⏱ 10.30-22.30. Adult: ¥1,500 / Child: ¥1,050 / Toddler: ¥530 / Under 3 free. ☎ 43-5751 💻 www.arm-manten.co.jp

♨ **Yakushima Green Hotel** (屋久島グリーンホテル) has a hot stone spa and onsen open to the general public. It is on the sea side of the main road at the northern end of Anbo. Price: ¥630. ⏱ 16.00-24.00. ☎ 46-3021 💻 yakushima-gh.com

♨ **JR Hotel Yakushima** (ＪＲホテル屋久島) is on the clifftop in Onoaida with great views out to sea from the huge onsen windows. There is a small outdoor section and all equipment - towels, soap, and shampoo - is provided. Again partly artificially heated though and the temperature is low at 34.7°C. ⏱ 15.00-18.00. Price: ¥1,000. ☎ 47-2011 💻 jrhotelgroup.com/eng/hotel/eng154.htm

♨ **Onoaida Onsen** (尾之間温泉) is at the start of the Onoaida mountain trail and has a foot bath outside for tired hikers, should you not wish to reveal all. It is signed towards the mountains at the main junction (the gas station is on one corner) in Onoaida and is at the end of the side road after 500 m. Get off at Onoaida Onsen entrance (尾之間温泉入口) bus stop and turn inland. It was discovered as a hot spring 350 years ago, is run by a spectacularly unfriendly woman and the bath is rather basic - you need to bring everything with you and can also get busy as it is free to use for Onoaida residents. It is however natural and piping hot (44-49°C). ⏱ 07.00-21.00 Price: Adult: ¥200 Child: ¥100. ☎ 47-2872

Onoaida Onsen

♨ **Hirauchi Seaside onsen** (平内海中温泉) is signed towards the sea from the main road between Hirauchi and Yudomari. Get off at Hirauchi kaichu onsen (平内海中温泉) bus stop. You need to choose your time to take this onsen as the sea can swallow it at high tide. There is a strict rule that bathers have to leave their clothes a few metres from the bath which can be embarrassing depending on the audience. Ladies should come equipped with a thin white towel to wrap around. There tends to be a steady stream of people who come to see the bath so for modest bathers it may feel a little uncomfortable. ⏱ 24 hours. ¥100 (in a donation box).

♨ **Yudomari Seaside onsen** (湯泊温泉) is signed towards the sea in Yudomari. Get off at Yudomari (湯泊) bus stop and walk down towards the sea. The road descends steeply and take a sharp left at the bottom to the car park. This onsen has more privacy and the male and female section has a bamboo screen between. There are toilets and changing rooms at the car park. Of the two outdoor onsens, Yudomari

is much better in its layout, although people will still come to gawk at you. There is also another even more private bath if you follow the path to the end. ⏱ 24 hours. ¥100 (in a donation box).

♨ **Hotel Tsuwanoya** (屋久島 つわのや) in Nagata has an artificially heated indoor/outdoor onsen open to the general public as well as its guests (in the accommodation section). ⏱ 15.00-21.00 Price: ¥525. ☎ 45-2717 🖥 tsuwanoya.com

10 PLACES OF INTEREST

Yakushima is blessed with stunning mountain ranges and world class hiking trails so when most people come to Yakushima they quite rightly head straight up the mountains, but there is more than meets the eye to the overgrown vegetation that lines the circular coastal road. The following section follows the circular coastal road clockwise from Miyanoura and on the way points out places of interest.

MIYANOURA AREA

Miyanoura

The village of Miyanoura (宮之浦) is the principal settlement on the island with more than 20% of Yakushima's population and is dominated by its two main industries: the Port and the silicon carbide factory owned by Yakushima Denko, an ugly collection of smoking rusty buildings on the hillside in the town centre. It is well worth wandering around to get the feel of the place but it is not the prettiest of villages – for beauty look beyond to the mountains. The

following sites in and around Miyanoura may be of interest:

YAKUSHIMA ENVIRONMENTAL CULTURE VILLAGE CENTER
(屋久島環境文化村センター)

Yakushima Environmental Culture Village Center

• On the corner of the main junction to the port. There is a car park at the rear.

• Get off at No.20 Miyanoura port entrance (宮之浦港入口) bus stop and walk towards the entrance of the port. Adults ¥500, High school/college ¥350, Elementary/Junior High ¥250 and under 6 are free. ⏰ 09.00-17.00. Closed on Mon. 💻 yakushima.or.jp/english ☎ 42-2900

If you want to get your bearings or if the weather takes a turn for the worse, this a nice little exhibition and has a 250-seat wide screen cinema showing a nature documentary of the island (shown about 8 times a day). It also serves as an information centre for hiking in the mountains and the staff should speak some English.

HISTORY AND FOLK MUSEUM
(屋久島町 歴史民俗資料館)

• Turn towards the mountains at the traffic signals north of Miyanoura river. Continue parallel to the river for 1 min and then it is on your left before you reach the end of the road.

• Get off at No.23 Miyanoura (宮之浦) bus stop and turn inland along the road running directly parallel to the river. (Do not cross the bridge). The museum is on your left after a 5 min walk.

The museum exhibits illustrate the history of the life of islanders and is an interesting detour if the weather keeps you off the mountains. Adults ¥100, Children ¥50. ⏰ 09.00-17.00 Closed Mon; from 12.00 on Sat, and on New Year holidays ☎ 42-5900

MIYANOURA RECREATIONAL PARK (屋久島総合自然公園)

• In Miyanoura, take the road heading to Shiratani Unsuikyo. Go past A co-op supermarket, cross the bridge and as the road curves there is a small parking area with drinking water on the right. The road next to this leads, after around a 5 min drive, to the car park on your right.

• Get off at No.31 Miyanoura Sho mae (宮之浦小) bus stop and take the mountain road towards Shiratani Unsuikyo. After crossing a river the road steeply rises and bends. Turn right at the sign for Miyanoura Recreational Park (屋久島総合自然公園) and the car park is at the end of the road (30 min).

There are essentially 2 parts to the park here, either side of the main road. One is the **Yaseishokubutsuen** (野生植物園) which is across the road from the car park, further away from the river. It has many of the plants and flowers that naturally

grow in Yakushima in greenhouses or display areas. ⏰ 8.30-17.00. Adults ¥300, Children ¥100. ☎ 42-2727

Miyanoura Recreational Park

The other part of the park surrounds the car park and is free of charge. It is nicely kept and there are two main paths that lead you around past the open air stage. The river next to the park can be found running along the far side. Find the wooden walkway and at some point you will find a gap in the trees so you can get to the rocks by the river. Have a dip in the crystal clear water or spot the odd monkey in the trees on the opposite bank, bring a picnic and relax. In late May, you may be lucky enough to see the thousands of fireflies that come out at night here in the park.

'KAMENKO' GLASS BOTTOMED BOAT
(海中展望船 かめんこ号)

• Park in the car park in Miyanoura port behind the park

• Get off at No.20 Miyanoura port entrance (宮之浦港入口) bus stop.

If you are not able to go snorkelling or scuba diving this is the next best thing for looking at life under the water around Yakushima. The boat has been modified so that you can see through the glass bottom and makes a short circular tour of the coral for 60 min. Adults ¥2,000 pp.⏰ Seasonal and depends on numbers ☎ 42-2300

ANBO AREA

PILLOW-SHAPED LAVA BEACH
(枕状溶岩)

• The beach is signed towards the sea 1 km south of Nagakubo village (永久保) and 4 km north of Anbo (安房). There is a small parking area where the two tracks start at the end of the road.

• Get off at No.57 Kuwano (桑野) bus stop then walk towards the sea at the turn-off.

The narrow road is lined by trees and after 700 m makes a sharp turn to the right. It then descends very steeply for 300 m as it winds itself down to the coast. At the bottom there are two tracks going in opposite directions. Left will take you 200 m to **Tashiro beach** (田代海岸) a quiet sandy beach, frequented by turtles in hatching season, and right 100 m to the fascinating lava rock formations.

The natural process of lava being cooled by the sea and then fresh lava breaking the newly formed crust and squeezing out more

boiling material have created what are supposed to look like folded pillows, hence the name.

Tashiro beach

ANBO (安房)

Anbo is the second main settlement after Miyanoura and has a thriving fishing port and farming industry. It is an interesting place to wander around and look at the weather beaten stores.

Head to the river area and you will pass a small shrine called Jochiku Tomari Mausoleum (如竹神社) dedicated to a Confucian scholar named **Jochiku Tomari**, the priest who has the dubious honour of encouraging local people to cut down their previously revered trees. (See 'the Forest' section for more details).

There is a local dance in Anbo which has been passed down generation to generation for 300 years called the Jochiku Odori dance to celebrate his actions.

ANBO PORT (安房港)

• Follow signs to the jet foil port and park in the car park nearby.

• Get off at No.64 Anbo port (安房港) bus stop.

This is home to the 'Toppy' jet foil but across from the pink terminal is one of the most important industries in Yakushima and in early afternoon is a hive of activity. This is the main fishing cooperative for 'Tobiuo' (飛び魚) otherwise known as flying fish. Over 1,000 tons of flying fish are caught here over the year and as much as 70% of all the flying fish sold in the markets of Japan are from here. There are over 30 different kinds of flying fish around Japan and most pass by Yakushima on the Kuroshio current but the most common types are the blue tobiuo (青トビウオ) and the 'semi' tobiuo (セミトビウオ). These can be found within 40 km from Yakushima's shores (See the 'Fauna' section for more details).

The Shige-maru. My old fishing boat.

ANBO RIVER (安房川)

• Anbo is at the mouth of the river. Parking is not easy around it though. Try the narrow river road near Manten bashi (the older of the two bridges) or find a place nearer the port and walk.

• Get off at No.66 Anbo (安房) bus stop and the river is very close.

The river is stunning in places and is so clear that the boulders deep below on the river bed appear as dark shadows.

Anbo river mouth

At the first sharp bend, there is a sand bank to the right (depending on the tide) and this is a good stopping point if only to swing on the rope and splash into the river.

Around the next bend, there is a channelled river which flows strongly from the left and the small stony beach area to the right is also a good stopping point.

The bridge ahead is the 75 m high **Matsumine O-hashi bridge** (松峯 大橋) - a local suicide spot - and all around is thick forest. Soon after you paddle under the bridge the rocks become larger and it is difficult to continue without carrying the kayak. It is still possible to continue but most people turn back soon after the bridge.

A flat boat, Anbo gawa Nagarebune (安房川流れ船), can also be hired for an evening cruise along the river.

HARUTAHAMA BEACH
(春田浜海水浴場)

• Signed on the main road near Anbo Bridge (安房橋). Turn towards the sea at the traffic signals and it is then a 5 min drive until a left turn at the small cement works. After 100 m there is a small car park next to the river.

• Get off at No.66 Anbo（安房）bus stop, walk across Anbo Bridge and turn left at the lights. Follow the road as it rises and then falls and continue parallel to the sea for 1.2 km until a left turn after the small cement works. The beach is then 100 m ahead.

Cross the small concrete bridge to the protected swimming area formed using the natural shape of the rocks. The pool has a life guard in the summer months and is a popular place to swim. The toilets and changing rooms are open July and August (09.30-17.30).

Harutahama beach

There is no sandy beach here but do not be put off - instead there is a carpet of jagged dead coral with rock pools full of fascinating sea creatures. Bring appropriate footware to clamber over the coral and head past the natural swimming pool to the area beyond.

YAKUSUGI MUSEUM
(屋久島町立屋久杉自然館)

• Take the mountain road to Yakusugiland (Route 592) for a few kilometers and you will be greeted with the large car park of Yakusugi museum on your left.

• Take any of the Yakusugiland/ Kigensugi or Arakawa buses. Get off at No.68 Yakusugi Shizenkan（屋久杉自然館）bus stop. The entrance is behind the trees. Adults ¥600, High school students ¥400, Junior High/ Elementary students ¥300 ⏰ 09.00-17.00 Closed on the 1st Tuesday of every month and New Year Holidays ☎ 46-3113.

The museum is set in large grounds with paths leading into a short circular forest walk. Inside it has displays about the forest including the 'Branch of life' exhibition（いのちの枝）featuring a branch from Jomon Sugi which snapped under the weight of snow in Dec 2005. There is also a pleasant cafe at the right entrance from the car park called Sugi-no-chaya（杉の茶屋）which is situated in thick forest.

Within the same grounds are two other buildings:

YAKUSHIMA WORLD HERITAGE CONSERVATION CENTRE
(屋久島世界遺産センター)

This free permanent exhibition has display panels and objects you can touch and feel related to the nature in Yakushima. It also serves as an information point for hiking and climbing in the mountains. If you are visiting the museum it is well worth the short walk. ⏰ 09.00-17.00 &

March - Nov open every day, Dec – Feb open every Sat, and closed for New Year Holidays. ① 46-2992 💻 yakushima.or.jp /English

YAKUSHIMA ENVIRONMENTAL CULTURE RESEARCH CENTRE

(屋久島環境文化研修センター)

This is next to the conservation centre and is not open to the general public. It provides lecture rooms, accommodation and educational facilities for groups learning about Yakushima and the environment. ① 46-2900 💻 yakushima.or.jp/english

SARU-KAWA GAJYUMARU

(猿川ガジュマル)

• About 1 km south of the village of Hirano (平野), there is a small wooden sign on the mountain side of the main road. Turn here and after 300 m there is a clearing in the forest on your right to park in.

• Get off at Nakabashi (中橋) and walk 300 m (Anbo direction) before turning left at the sign or get off at Shouchugawa (焼酎川) and walk 500 m (Onoaida direction) before turning right.

Follow the small path to the end and it should lead you to the famous Gajyumaru or Banyan trees to your right. They are very distinctive in appearance because their aerial roots hang down to the ground like tentacles.

ONOAIDA AREA

YAKUSHIMA BOTANICAL RESEARCH PARK

(ボタニカルリサーチパーク)

• A few min south of Mugio (麦生), it is clearly signed on the left and the entrance to the car park is from the main road.

• Get off at No.86 Research park (リサーチパーク) bus stop and it is in front of you, on the sea side of the road.

Popular with tour groups as it also has a restaurant, it displays the range of subtropical to temperate zone plants, fruits and herbs in Yakushima. Open: March-Aug 09.00 - 18.30 / Sept-Feb 09.00- 16.00 but closed on New Year Holidays. Adults ¥1,000 / Student ¥800 / Child ¥500. ① 47-2636.

TOROKI-NO-TAKI WATERFALL

(トローキの滝)

• Just south of Mugio (麦生) and before the large red bridge, there is a tiny path on the sea side of the road to view Toroki-no-taki. You can park opposite in the car park of the 'Pontankan' (ポンタン館) centre.

• Get off at No.87 Tainokawa (鯛ノ川) bus stop and look for the stone sign marking the path on the sea-side of the road.

There is not that much to see apart from the waterfall in the distance and you might have to crane your neck to see through the bushes but it is one of only two waterfalls in the whole of Japan to flow directly into the sea.

The height of the waterfall is an unspectacular 6 m but if you follow the path to the end, the mountain backdrop (Mochomu dake) and the bridge just behind make it all the more impressive

Toroki-no-taki Waterfall

The 'Pontankan' (ポンタン館) building in the car park across the road has toilets and sells locally grown food and locally made souvenirs.

SENPIRO-NO-TAKI WATERFALL

(千尋の滝)

• Follow the signs heading inland at Hara (原). There are several routes from the main road all leading to the same windy 3 km road. Midway it makes a tight right turn but continue past the ponkan orchards and keep climbing until you reach the car park and souvenir store.

• Get off at any one of 3 bus stops in or near Hara. Either get off at N.87 Tainokawa (鯛ノ川) bus stop and walk 300 m across the bridge to the signed right turn; Or get off at No.88 Hara Iriguchi (原入口) and walk (Onoaida direction) until the park where you turn right; Or get off at No.89 Hara (原) and walk (Anbo

direction) to the park where you turn left. Whichever stop you get off at it is 2.3 km to the waterfall and 1.5 km before the waterfall the road makes a sharp right turn.

Follow the 100 m path to a viewing area some distance from the 60 m high falls. From there you can see (weather permitting) the most impressive feature of the waterfall and that is the granite that it flows on.

It is one solid piece of granite rock measuring somewhere between 200 m x 400 m and as such is the largest single piece in Japan. Senpiro (千尋) gets its name from the measurement of the distance between your hands if you stand with your arms outstretched. This measurement is called one hiro (一尋). The size of the granite was therefore described as the size of 1,000 people standing arms outstretched side by side, hence 'Senpiro' ('Sen' [千]= 1,000 and 'piro'[尋] = measurement).

Senpiro-no-taki Waterfall

You could once walk up to the waterfall but the path was closed due to the deaths of 3 hikers in a flash flood when trying to cross the river with their guide in 2003. The lookout point is usually busy with tourists as it is so accessible, but is worth seeing purely for that spectacularly large chunk of granite.

YAMANKO YUSUI SPRING WATER （山河湧水）

Yamanko Yusui Spring

• On the mountain side of the main road in No.89 Hara （原）, at the bridge midway through the village. Either side of the park there are side roads to stop in.

• Get off at Hara （原） bus stop and walk [Anbo direction] to the park on the mountain side of the main road.

This small park, Yamanko koen （山河公園）, has picnic areas and a stream running through it. At the back of the park is bamboo piped spring water allowing you to fill up the bamboo cups provided with fresh cool mountain water from Mochomu dake.

♨ HIRAUCHI SEASIDE ONSEN （平内海中温泉）

• Turn towards the sea at the sign between Hirauchi and Yudomari. After 500 m there is a turning and a very small car park.

• Get off either at No.113 Nishikaikon （西開墾） or No.112 Hirauchi kaichu onsen （平内海中温泉）

bus stops and head towards the sea for 500 m where the road curves around and there is the path to the onsen.

♨ YUDOMARI SEASIDE ONSEN （湯泊温泉）

• Turn towards the sea at the sign on the main road in Yudomari village. After 200 m, turn left (the 3rd left) and then after another 200 m take a sharp left and the car park is in front.

• Get off at No.114 Yudomari （湯泊） bus stop and walk (Kurio direction) to the signed turning towards the sea. After 200 m, turn left (the 3rd left) and then after another 200 m take a sharp left and the entrance is ahead.

More details on both of these seaside onsens are in the hot springs section.

KURIO AREA

NAKAMA BEACH （中間浜） and NAKAMA GAJYUMARU （中間ガジュマル）

• Nakama is 3 km south of Kurio. Both sides of the road here are lined with low concrete walls but there is a gravel parking area at the far end of the beach. There is also a small parking area near the Gajyumaru, 200 m inland from the main road.

• Get off at No.123 Nakama （中間） bus stop and the beach is in front. Walk for about 100 m (Kurio direction) and turn inland then follow the road through Nakama for 300 m to the Gajyumaru.

The beach is accessible through gaps in the sea wall. It is made up of coarse grained sand and often frequented by turtles in nesting season. The collection of Gajyumaru is worth a side trip if only to see how the vines weave an archway over the road.

YAKUSHIMA FRUIT GARDEN
(屋久島フルーツガーデン)

• Turn inland just east of Nakama River and take either the first or second right. The way is clearly signed.

• Get off at No.123 Nakama (中間) bus stop and walk back 200 m across the river. Take the first left and continue on next to the river, past Nakama Gajyumaru (中間ガジュマル) on your left across the bridge, and take the next right after that (about a 20 min walk).

Adults ¥500 / Children ¥250. Around 1,600 types of tropical fruits and plants are grown here and you are guided around in a group (only in Japanese). At the end of the tour you also get to taste a selection of the seasonal fruit. ⏰ 08.00-17.00 ☎ 48-2468

KURIO BEACH (栗生浜海水浴場)

• The car park is just as you reach Kurio (from Onoaida). On the left there is an old fishing boat perched beside a small cafe. Turn left straight after it.

• Get off at No.125 Kurio Iriguchi (栗生入口) bus stop and walk (Onoaida direction) for 1 min. It is on the right.

This is a small sandy beach at the mouth of Kurio River. It is bordered either side by the concrete blocks of the harbour to prevent the beach being eroded. There is a concrete shelter at the top of the beach for shade and the changing rooms next to the toilets are open in July and August (09.00-18.00). It is a popular, safe beach for swimming and is frequented by turtles in hatching season.

NATURAL MANGROVE SITE
(メヒルギ自生地区)

Natural Mangrove site

• Park before Kurio bridge (on the opposite side to Kurio village) at the side of the main road. Then follow the track that runs beside the river towards the sea.

• Get off at No.127 Kurio bashi (栗生橋) bus stop. Take the track by the river heading towards the sea. At the end of the track follow the path to a stone sign and the mangroves are in the water nearby.

This site is recognised as an example of a rare distribution of the mangrove tree species. Mangroves are common in the southern islands of the Ryukyu chain but not normally found at this latitude. The trees themselves have rooted on the riverside sandbank and bloom from late summer with a white 5 petalled flower.

SHAKUNAGE FOREST PARK
(石楠花の森公園)

• Turn right after Kurio bridge at the sign and take the single track road through small landholdings to the end where there is a car park.

• Get off at No.127 Kurio bashi (栗生橋) bus stop and walk inland on the single track road.

The best time to visit here is in the rhododendron flowering season which is from April to June.

The trail leads on a wooden walkway beside Kurio river and then opens out into a large garden brimmed full with rhododendrons and with access to the river. It is very beautiful around the crystal clear river and both sides are bordered by thick forest. ⏱ April to Aug: 09.00-18.30/Sept to March: 09.00-16.00. Adults ¥500 / Children ¥250.

Rhododendrons at Shakunage Forest Park

TSUKASAKI TIDE POOL
(塚崎タイドプール)

• Go across Kurio bridge and continue up the hill towards Oko-notaki waterfall. It is signed to the left on the bend. Go through Yakushima Youth Travel village (屋久島青少年旅行村) and at the end, take the single track road to the left which runs beside the mouth of Kurio river. At the end of that there is a small car park in front of a picnic shelter and a basic shower block.

Tsukasaki tide pool

• Get off at No.128 Seishonen-mura (青少年村) bus stop and walk down through Yakushima Youth Travel village.

Tsukasaki tide pool refers to the rock pools around this headland but the largest of them begins adjacent to here and depending on what time of day you reach it, is a perfect place to go snorkelling. At low tide it is still possible to snorkel but it is at its best when relatively full with water as the fish are so plentiful. The pool is at the river mouth and bordered by rocks apart from the opening in the far corner closest to the sea. The closer you snorkel to here, the more fish there should be. Watch out for the colourful trigger fish which, despite their small size, may nip at you. Its position at the mouth of Kurio river means that visibility however can sometimes be affected as the fresh and salt water mix.

OKO YUSUI MOUNTAIN SPRING WATER (大川湧水)

Shortly before Oko-no-taki waterfall there is a lay-by on the mountain side of the main road. Stop here and you will see a wooden sign and a small spring. The water is drinkable and straight from the mountain river.

OKO-NO-TAKI WATERFALL
(大川の滝)

• Signed inland at a bend on the main road, 4 km north of Kurio. A single lane track leads you 200 m across a small concrete bridge and there is a very small car park immediately to the left. If necessary park at a safe place on the roadside going up under the large bridge.

• Get off at No.129 Oko-no-taki (大川の滝) bus stop (the final destination) and it is a 300 m walk to the waterfall. The bus stop is close to Oko spring water above.

The size and volume of water of this 88 m high waterfall makes it the largest in Yakushima and the highest in southern Kyushu. The information sign will tell you that it has been selected as one of 'the best 100 waterfalls in Japan' and the water pool in front of the waterfall has also been selected as one of 'the best 100 bodies of water in Japan'.

There is a concrete walkway by the side of the river which ends at a concrete picnic table and from then on clamber over the rocks for a closer look. If you arrive around 3pm a rainbow is sometimes visible in the spray.

It depends on the time of year as to how impressive Oko-no-taki can be. In times of low rainfall the water trickles down but in the rainy season the valley is a raging torrent. The whole 20-metre-wide rock face gushes water, smothering the concrete pathway and picnic table completely and threatening to reach the height of the bridge. It is only when the river is seen at its fiercest that you can understand how the giant boulders that stand in the valley were originally brought there.

Oko-no-taki

The river continues on for around 500 m to the sea and is accessible via a path leading down to a small toilet block. Continue along the stony track and you will arrive after 5 min at Sagoshi-no-hama (サゴシの浜), a secluded bay at the mouth of the river.

SEIBU RINDO FOREST PATH
(西部林道)

On the west side of the island the World Heritage Site Protection Area extends all the way down to the seashore and the Seibu Rindo road cuts its way through this thick forest between Nagata and Kurio. From both directions the road rises steeply with plenty of blind forested bends and continues like this for a windy 26½ km until the descent down to the coast.

As the single track road rises towards Kuniwari dake (国割岳) there are many scenic vantage points of the forest allowing you to see how the distribution of trees clearly changes both in colour and shape with altitude. It also is very common to spot troops of macaques and deer on or beside the road.

Seibu Rindo Forest Path

No buses run this route so options are limited without a car or motorbike, but with a little planning it is perfectly feasible by bicycle or on foot. There are plans to expand the road to make a complete circular road around the island which of course will have a major impact on the fragile environment that exists here if followed through.

NAGATA AREA

YAKUSHIMA LIGHTHOUSE
(屋久島灯台)

• Yakushima lighthouse is to the North West of the island at

Nagatamisaki (永田岬). It is on the edge of the Seibu Rindo path and is signed 5 km west of Nagata. Take the side road for 1 km until the car park at the end.

There has been a lighthouse here since 1897 to protect the main ship routes in the deep waters to the north west of the island. The actual lighthouse itself is nothing special but there are beautiful views of Kuchierabu (口永良部島) island and other more distant islands from the cliff top. It is also a good place to see the blooming pink flower of the Marubasatsuki or Azalea plants in early summer.

NAGATA RIVER (永田川) and YOKKO VALLY (横河渓谷)

• Turn inland just before Nagata Bridge (永田橋) at the gas station and keep parallel to the river. This may mean taking a left turn depending on which way you came from. Continue parallel to the river for 1 km to the small bridge to the left (do not cross it) and follow the road up for a further 300 m. There will be an old weathered sign and a small turning to the left into the Nagata trail car park.

• Get off at No.1 Nagata (永田) bus stop and walk inland parallel to the river. After 1 km a bridge crosses the river to your left, do not cross it but continue for a further 300 m to the car park of the trail. (30 min walk).

From the beginning of the Nagata trail (永田歩道) follow the paved path until it becomes forest floor and carefully hop over a stream.

After 6 min there is a naturally formed swimming area complete with a slippery rock waterslide on your left. This is known as Yokogawa or locally as Yokko valley (横河渓谷). You get a few glimpses of it through the trees before you reach the collection of rocks that lead you down to the river. In the summer months it is a popular spot for a picnic or to take a dip in the crystal clear water. On a safety note, visit here with caution after heavy rains as like many of Yakushima's rivers, it is prone to flash floods.

Yokogawa natural pool

NAGATA INAKAHAMA BEACH
(永田いなか浜)

• Less than 1 km north of Nagata village. Park in any of the gravel lay-bys next to the beach.

• Get off at No.4 Inakahama (いなか浜) bus stop.

This is the longest stretch of sandy beach on the island. From May to July it is the focal point of loggerhead turtle egg laying activity and nesting areas are usually roped off with bamboo posts and signs. Care should be taken not to climb over any barriers erected as these are to protect newly laid legs from being trampled. At sundown the beach is patrolled by volunteers monitoring the turtles. Outside of this time however there are no restrictions and the beach is a welcome relief from the forest all around.

Inakahama beach

SEA TURTLE CENTRE
(うみがめ館)

• On the mountain side of the road, mid-way along Inakahama beach (いなか浜) in Nataga. Park in the beach-side car park.

• Get off at No.5 Nakanobashi (中野橋) bus stop and walk 200 m (Nagata village direction) or get off at No.4 Inakahama (いなか浜) bus stop and walk 200 m (Isso direction). The centre is across the street from the beach. Adults ¥200 / Students ¥100.

This is run by the Yakushima Umigame Center (屋久島 うみがめ館), a Non-Profit Organisation (NPO) set up to protect the sea turtles on Nagata's beaches. The centre has shells, models, pictures and maps of turtle activity around Yakushima and information on some of the exhibits is in both Japanese and English. ⊙ All year (Closed on Tuesdays) 09.00-17.00. During the nesting and hatching seasons it opens at night ☎ 49-6550 🖥 umigame-kan.org

There are two important events that take place every year here and if you are lucky enough to be in Yakushima at these times, you get the chance to see the turtles in action:

TURTLE EGG LAYING

From mid-May to the end of July, Inakahama beach becomes a hive of activity at night. The focal point is in the collection of huts just in front of the beach, a short distance from the turtle centre. ⏰ May 15th to July 31st 20.30-23.00 Adults: ¥800, Students: ¥500, Children: ¥300. ☎ 090-8768-4281 FAX 45-2484 🖥 umigame.refire.jp

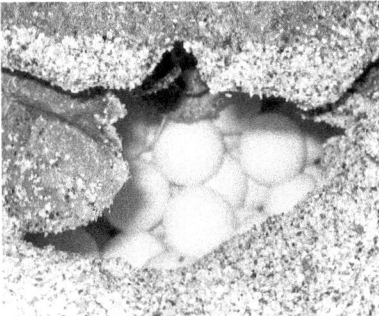

Turtle eggs being laid

The number of visitors has been restricted to 80 per night so you need to reserve your place in advance in order not to be turned away. This can be done though your accommodation, directly or through the tourist information offices. Most of staff you see are local volunteers and part of the NPO (but not necessarily friendly). Pay in the admin hut and then wait for the first part of the evening which is a talk on turtles, swiftly followed by a documentary on a turtle named 'Jane' (ジェーン) who periodically returns to Yakushima (all in Japanese). After that you have to wait. The turtles could come at any time so the wait could be long or short and there are some nights when no turtle comes at all in which case you get your money back.

If you are lucky it will be a short wait before one is spotted laying eggs and you are told to follow one of the volunteer guides. This could be right in front of the hut on the beach or it could be 1 km away on one of the other beaches.

When you reach the egg laying turtle, the guide will shine a torch and explain (in Japanese) about the process. It takes around an hour before the turtle is finished and flips sand back into the hole to seal it. It will then drag itself back into the sea and the show ends.

It is forbidden to take photos with a flash and to get too close while with the turtle for obvious reasons.

HATCHING OF BABY TURTLES

August 1st to August 31st 20.00-21.30. Adults and High/Junior High school students: ¥200 Elementary school students and under: ¥100.

This begins with a lecture about the turtles in the turtle centre (in Japanese) and then a trip across the road to the beach where staff will release baby turtles and you can observe them struggle along the beach to the sea.

These baby turtles are hatched from eggs collected by the centre from vulnerable parts of the beach in the egg laying season a few months before. They are no longer at risk of being dug up for food – the consumption of turtle eggs was banned in Yakushima in 1973 and then later in 1988 in Kagoshima Prefecture. But they are at risk of being trampled underfoot or being eaten by scavengers like the recently introduced raccoon dog.

ISSO AREA

FUIN-NO-TAKI WATERFALL
(布引の滝)

This has a car park, immaculate toilets and rest area and is on the main by-pass road at Isso, 200 m from Isso Bridge. The closest bus stop is No.12 Isso Iriguchi (一 湊入口). The water is little more than a trickle unless after heavy rain when it becomes very impressive.

ISSO BEACH (一湊海水浴場)

Isso beach

• Signed just East of Isso on the main road. Look for the car park.

• Get off at No.13 Yahazu (矢筈) bus stop which is close to the car park.

A large triangular picnic shelter and a concrete frame of a building lead on to a steep sandy beach. In the summer months it is one of the most popular swimming sites with

beach/swim equipment for rent and refreshments in temporary huts.

There are concrete blocks laid on the sea bed 200 m out which reduces wave impact on the beach. The shower blocks open in July and August (09.00-18.00).

From the beach you may be able to see a red Torii (鳥居) gate on the right headland. This marks the entrance to Isso Yahazudake Shrine (一湊矢筈嶽神社) and the access road is the side road which runs east of the main road behind the car park. The sign says Yahazu Park (矢筈公園) and if you take the left fork, it will take you to the start of the path marked by another red gate. It is a short walk to the shrine which is hidden at the back of a dark cave. A local story tells of a cat which got lost in this cave while chasing a mouse, only to reappear some time later in Kumano shrine in Tanegashima island.

If you then take the road to the end of the headland. There is a car park, the remains of Yahazu Park's recreational area which has now overgrown but there is still a footpath to the cliffs with views out to sea.

SHITOKO GAJYUMARU PARK
(志戸子 ガジュマル園)

• Signed from the main road at Shitogo (志戸子), 3 km east of Isso. Turn towards the sea, after 200 m turn right and then the park is 300 m ahead. The road is narrow and the car park is next to the sea wall in front of the park.

• Get off at No.14 Shitoko (志戸子) bus stop and walk 200 m towards the sea. At the junction turn right and the park is 300 m to the right. Adults ¥200 / Students ¥100.

Some of the banyan trees here are as old as 500 years and there are plenty of specimens to look at in this small park. There is a Gajyumaru festival held outside the park in May with local food to try. ⏱ April-August 08.30-18.30 Sept-March 08.30-17.00 ☎ 42-0100

Shitoko Gajyumaru Park

11 WATER ACTIVITIES

Swimming

Sea: The most popular spots to swim in the sea are at Inakahama beach, Isso beach, Harutahama in Anbo and Kurio beach. Be aware especially at Inakahama that off-shore currents run close to the beach so swim out with caution. In the other beaches safe areas have been designated and have life guards in the summer months.

River: Miyanoura river at Miyanoura Recreational Park, Nagata river at Yokogawa and Anbo river are also good for swimming in the summer months.

Canoeing/Kayaking

Kayaking along Yakushima's rivers offers rewarding and often stunning views of the forest and mountains. Rental canoes and kayaks are usually available near Anbo river although many companies now prefer to offer guide services. Tourist information centres can often help with reservations.

A 2-3 hour canoeing trip in Anbo river with a guide ranges from ¥6,000-¥8,000. To rent a kayak without the guide costs ¥3,000-¥5,000 for 1 or ¥5,000-¥8,000 for 2 depending if you want ½ day or a full day.

• ☺ **Blue Water Kayaks Yakushima** (ブルーウォーターカヤックス屋久島) in Shitoko offers a day kayak with lunch ① 49-1290/090-5727-2426

🖳 www8.ocn.ne.jp/~kayaks 🗐 bluewater-yakushima@ blue.ocn.ne.jp

• **Yakushima Field Guide SPINNAKER** (屋久島 フィールドガイド スピニカ) is in Anbo and offers full and half day trips. ① 46-3223 🖳 http://yakushima-kayak.com 🗐 spinnaker@yakushima-kayak.com

• **Canoe House Yakushima** (カヌーハウス屋久島) in Onoaida offers canoeing on Anbo river and also sea kayaking around Toroki falls.① 47-2559 / 090-2397-9653 contact Miyatsukasa-san. 🖳 homepage3.nifty.com/~yakushima/sub1.htm

• ☺ **Yakushima Kayaker KAZE** (屋久島カヤックツアーＫＡＺＥ) is a qualified kayak specialist and offers day trips. ① 46-2989 🖳 www11.ocn.ne.jp/~kayaq 🗐 kayaknavigator_kaze@wing. ocn.ne.jp

Scuba diving

For anyone who has never dived before, there are plenty of companies offering supervised diving with an instructor. Prices range from ¥10,000 – ¥11,000 for ½ day (1 dive) and ¥15,000 – ¥16,000 for a full day (2 dives). Each session lasts around 3 hours but the dive itself is for 30 min and descends to 4-6 m under the water. The rest of the time is spent in safety training.

All companies offer a pick-up service from your accommodation and include insurance, equipment, tax and a soft drink. For full day trips you need your own lunch. You will need a swimsuit, a change of clothes and shampoo/soap/towel. The tourist information or your accommodation can help organise this or try the following companies (basic knowledge of Japanese may be required):

• **Ever Blue Yakushima** (エバーブルー屋久島) in Miyanoura offers certified PADI training as well as short dives. ☎ 42-0505 💻 yakushima-diving.com/eng.html ✉ eby@yakushima-diving.com

• **Yakushima Diving Station Maru** (屋久島ダイビングステーションまる) ☎ 49-1919/090-8663-4167 in Kusugawa. 💻 maru-yakushima.net ✉ maru@maru-yakushima.net

• **Yakushima Guide Club** (屋久島ガイドクラブ) in Anbo offers kayaking and diving. ☎46-3160 💻yakushima-guide.jp ✉ club@yakushima-guide.jp

For experienced divers who just want to rent the equipment. The prices are around ¥500 each for a mask, snorkel, fins and boots, and BC, regulator and wet suit around ¥1,500 each. You can rent the lot for ¥5,000. (The gloves are free)

Snorkelling

There are many places you can snorkel around Yakushima but the popular (and relatively safe) places with a wide selection of underwater sights are:

• At Isso in **Motoura** (元浦) bay (the bay east of Isso beach)

• **Harutahama** beach in Anbo (where the river meets the sea)

• **Yudomari port** (head towards the seaside Onsen but when at the water's edge do not turn left to the onsen but continue 500 m straight on to the end of the road and then

walk over the rocks to the right of the harbour wall)

• **Tsukasaki tide pool** in Kurio.

Bring or buy a snorkel, although they can be rented in some locations. **Canoe House Yakushima** (カヌーハウス屋久島) for example offers a mask, snorkel, fins, and boots for ¥2,000 for the whole day. Some kind of sea footwear is a must and if you are anywhere near rocks wear gloves.

If you would prefer, it is possible to organise a snorkeling trip with a guide for around ¥10,000 plus equipment rental (this would be around ¥2,000) at **Yakushima Diving Station Maru** (details above).

Fishing

Fishing is a popular past-time with the locals in Yakushima so finding supplies and equipment is relatively easy. Some's store in Koseda and Yakuden Life Centre in Miyanoura sell a range of fishing equipment and there are many smaller specialized stores.

Canoe House (see above for details) offers supervised fishing trips in the early morning or at night in Onoaida for ¥6,000 per person.

12 CRAFT ACTIVITIES

Yakushima is famous for two crafts: its Yakusugi woodcraft and its Yakushimayaki pottery. Both can be bought is many stores on the island but you can also have a go at making them yourself.

Making Yakusugi woodcraft

There are many places on the island where you can, with supervision, make your own objects from yakusugi wood. This could be anything from 45 min to 2 hours depending on what you make. The most common objects are key chains and chopsticks. Here are some of the larger companies which offer this service:

A chopstick class at Kashima Kougei

• **Kashima Kougei** (鹿島工芸) is on the hill leading south out of Anbo. They do not speak English but are very friendly and will teach you how to make chopsticks. If you wish to buy raw Yakusugi wood to take home with you go to and there is usually a large pile of wood for sale outside the workshop. All pieces are priced and if no one is there put the money in the container provided. TEL: 46-2613

• **Suginoya** (杉の舎本店) is in Koseda very close to the airport. You can make chopsticks in about 50 min. Booking is required ① 43-5441.

• **Sugisho** (杉匠) is on the main road in Anbo after the first main junction (coming from Miyanoura). You can make keychains and chopsticks for ¥1,500 (45 min), pendants, saucers

and mouse pads for ¥2,500 (45 min) and larger objects like mugs and plates for up to ¥5,000. ① 46-2123 ⌨ hidakataka@able.ocn.ne.jp

• **Takedasangyo** (武田産業) is just before the same junction in Anbo and offers a workshop tour as well as making chopsticks. 🖥 yakusugitakeda.com ① 46-2258

If you wish to buy raw Yakusugi wood to take home with you go to **Kashima Kougei** (鹿島工芸) and there is usually a large pile of wood for sale outside the workshop. All pieces are priced and if no one is there put the money in the container provided. ① 46-2613.

Making Yakushima pottery

Yakushimayaki Shimpachinogama

(屋久島焼新八野［シンパチノ］窯) ① 47-2624 is in Hirauchi, is the original 'Yakushima' pottery and the oldest potter's on the island. They use iron-rich Yakushima clay and bake in a firewood kiln that includes ash and weathered coral to give a unique finish. It offers supervised pottery making by hand from ¥2,000 or by potter's wheel from ¥2,500 ⏰ 15.00-18.00. You need to book beforehand. English is spoken.

The sign for the pottery is 200 m after the turn off for Hirauchi Seaside Onsen (平内海中温泉) on the mountain side of the main road (heading towards Kurio).

By bus get off at Nishikaikon (西開墾) bus stop and head inland. The pottery is a short distance on the left. 🖥 www6.ocn.ne.jp/~yakugama

BUS TIMETABLES

Each Yakushima Kostu bus stop (the bus stop sign on the right) has a number on it which corresponds to the number in the columns of the timetable. In this case you can see 72 which means that it is the Kigensugi bus stop. The Matsubanda sign (the sign on the left) is not numbered here but uses the same stop numbers.

A. ARAKAWA TRAIL ENTRANCE BUS

(1st March - 30th November)

(Free pass not accepted)

Yakusugi Museum to Arakawa Trail					
68	Leaves Museum	04.40	05.00	05.30	06.00	13.00
70	Arrives at Arakawa	05.20	05.40	06.10	06.40	13.40

Arakawa Trail Entrance to Yakusugi Museum								
70	Leaves Arakawa	07.00	14.00	15.00	16.00	16.30	17.00	17.30	18.00
68	Arrives at Museum	07.40	14.40	15.40	16.40	17.10	17.40	18.10	18.40

NOTE: Remember that you have to buy your ticket beforehand. One way for an adult is ¥850 and the tickets can be bought in tourist information centers, convenience stores, climbing gear shops, souvenir shops, taxi companies, lots of accommodations and with guides.

B. YAKUSUGILAND & KIGENSUGI ROUTE

(屋久杉ランド)   (紀元杉線)

1. YAKUSHIMA KOUTSU

(Free pass OK)

No	Gochomae to Kigensugi			No	Kigensugi to Gochomae		
62	Gochomae (Anbo)	09:16	13.26	72	Kigensugi	10.39	14.49
64	Anbo Port		13.31	71	Yakusugiland	10.59	15.09
66	Anbo	09.20	13.33	69	Arakawa junction	11.05	15.15
67	Makino	09.21	13.34	68	Yakusugi museum	11.32	15.42
68	Yakusugi museum	09.26	13.39	67	Makino	11.37	15.47
69	Arakawa junction	09.53	14.06	66	Anbo	11.38	15.48
71	Yakusugiland	09.59	14.12	64	Anbo Port		
72	Kigensugi	10.19	14.35	62	Gochomae (Anbo)	11.42	15.52

* Gochomae is the bus terminal in Anbo north of the main part of town on route 77.

2. MATSUBANDA KOUTSU

(Free pass not accepted)

Miyanoura ↔ Kigensugi

20	Miyanoura Port	12.40	72	Kigensugi	16.21
19	Culure Center	12.40	71	Yakusugiland	16.39
21	Port Entrance	12.41	69	Arakawa Junction	16.44
22	Noboriagari	12.42	68	Yakusugi museum	17.11
23	Miyanoura	12.43	67	Makino	17.16
24	Miyanoura shisho	12.44	66	Anbo	17.17
25	Oharamachi	12.44	65	Nakaiin mae	17.18
30	Outside A coop	12.45	64	Anbo Port	17.19
31	Miyanourasho mae	12.46	65	Nakaiin mae	17.20
32	Koukou mae	12.47	63	Keisatsusho mae	17.21
33	Eidan	12.48	62	Gochomae	17.22
34	Asahimachi	12.48	61	Chuuou	17.22
35	Torigoe	12.49	60	Isobe	17.23
36	Kusugawa Iriguchi	12.50	59	Funayuki	17.25
37	Kusugawa	12.50	58	Ryuuten	17.26
38	Yunokawa onsen	12.52	57	Kuwano	17.27
42	Otokogawa	12.56	56	Nagakubo	17.28
43	Nishi Koseda	12.57	49	Airport (Kuukou)	17.33
48	Outside airport	13.01	48	Outside airport	17.33
49	Airport (Kuukou)	13.01	43	Nishi Koseda	17.37
56	Nagakubo	13.06	42	Otokogawa	17.48
57	Kuwano	13.07	38	Yunokawa onsen	17.42
59	Funayuki	13.09	37	Kusugawa	17.44
60	Isobe	13.11	36	Kusugawa Iriguchi	17.44
61	Chuuou	13.12	35	Torigoe	17.45
62	Gochomae	13.12	34	Asahimachi	17.46
63	Keisatsusho mae	13.13	33	Eidan	17.46
65	Nakaiin mae	13.14	32	Koukou mae	17.47
64	Anbo Port	13.15	31	Miyanourasho mae	17.48
65	Nakaiin mae	13.16	30	Outside A coop	17.49
66	Anbo	13.17	25	Oharamachi	17.50
67	Makino	13.18	24	Miyanoura shisho	17.50
68	Yakusugi museum	13.23	23	Miyanoura	17.51
69	Arakawa junction	13.48	22	Noboriagari	17.52
71	Yakusugiland	13.53	21	Port Entrance	17.53
72	Kigensugi	14.11	19	Culture Center	17.54
			20	Miyanoura Port	17.54

C. SHIRATANI UNSUIKYO ROUTE （白谷雲水峡線）

1. YAKUSHIMA KOUTSU

(Free pass OK)

No	Miyanoura Port to Shiratani					No	Shiratani to Miyanoura Port				
20	Miyanoura Port	08.20	10.00	13.30	15.30	29	Shiratani Unsuikyo	09.00	11.00	14.40	16.10
21	Port Entrance	08.26	10.06	13.36	15.36	28	Kumo-no-tenbodai	09.10	11.10	14.50	16.20
23	Miyanoura	08.28	10.08	13.38	15.38	27	Mori-no-tenbodai	09.13	11.13	14.53	16.23
25	Oharamachi	08.29	10.09	13.39	15.39	26	Ushitoko koen	09.23	11.23	15.03	16.33
26	Ushitoko koen	08.32	10.12	13.42	15.42	25	Oharamachi	09.26	11.26	15.06	16.36
27	Mori-no-tenbodai	08.42	10.22	13.52	15.52	23	Miyanoura	09.27	11.27	15.07	16.37
28	Kumo-no-tenbodai	08.45	10.25	13.55	15.55	21	Port Entrance	09.29	11.29	15.09	16.39
29	Shiratani Unsuikyo	08.55	10.35	14.05	16.05	20	Miyanoura Port	09.35	11.35	15.15	16.45

2. MATSUBANDA KOUTSU

(Free pass not accepted)

No	Miyanoura Port to Shiratani				No	Shiratani to Miyanoura Port			
20	Miyanoura Port	08.00[A]	11.20	13.00	29	Shiratani Unsuikyo	09.30	12.00	15.10
21	Port Entrance	08.02	11.20	13.00	28	Kumo-no-tenbodai	09.39	12.09	15.19
22	Noboriagari	08.03	11.23	13.02	27	Mori-no-tenbodai	09.42	12.12	15.22
23	Miyanoura	08.04	11.24	13.04	26	Ushitoko koen	09.51	12.21	15.31
24	Miyanoura shisho	08.05	11.25	13.05	25	Oharamachi	09.55	12.25	15.35
25	Oharamachi	08.05	11.25	13.05	24	Miyanoura shisho	09.55	12.25	15.35
26	Ushitoko koen	08.09	11.29	13.09	23	Miyanoura	09.56	12.26	15.36
27	Mori-no-tenbodai	08.18	11.38	13.18	22	Noboriagari	09.57	12.27	15.37
28	Kumo-no-tenbodai	08.21	11.41	13.21	21	Port Entrance	09.58	12.28	15.38
29	Shiratani Unsuikyo	08.30	11.50	14.30	20	Miyanoura Port	10.00	12.30[B]	15.40[C]

[A] and [C] connect with Matsubanda buses to Anbo (See Anbo-Miyanoura route)

[B] connects with the Matsubanda bus to Kigensugi (See Miyanoura-Kigensugi route

D. YAKUSHIMA KOTSU COASTAL ROUTE (Free pass OK)

Nagata – Miyanoura – Airport – Anbo – Onoaida – Kurio-bashi - Oko-no-taki

Notes: [1] Not at weekends or on holidays · [2] March to November only

No	Destination	Museum	Anbo Port	Kurio-bashi[1]	Makino[1]	Kurio-bashi	Oko-no-taki	Iwasaki Hotel	Kurio-bashi	Kurio-bashi	Iwasaki Hotel	Oko-no-taki	Iwasaki Hotel	Oko-no-taki	Iwasaki Hotel	Kurio-bashi	Kaichu onsen[2]	Iwasaki Hotel	Kurio-bashi
1	Nagata	04.30				07.26		09.26	10.20	10.41	11.31	12.50	13.26	15.25	15.11	16.45		17.01	18.10
4	Inakahama	04.31				07.28		09.28	10.21	10.43	11.33	12.51	13.28	15.26	15.13	16.46		17.03	18.11
8	Yoshida	04.33				07.36		09.36	10.23	10.51	11.41	12.53	13.36	15.28	15.21	16.48		17.11	18.13
11	Isso	04.34				07.42		09.42	10.24	10.57	11.47	12.54	13.42	15.29	15.27	16.49		17.17	18.14
14	Shitoko	04.36				07.47		09.47	10.26	11.02	11.52	12.56	13.47	15.31	15.32	16.51		17.22	18.16
17	Futagawa	04.37	05.54			07.54		09.54	10.27	11.09	11.59	12.57	13.54	15.32	15.39	16.52		17.29	18.17
20	Miyanoura Port	04.39	06.00			08.00	08.40	10.00	10.29	11.15	12.05	12.59	14.00	15.34	15.45	16.54		17.35	18.19
21	Port Entrance	04.41	06.01			08.01	08.41	10.01	10.31	11.16	12.06	13.01	14.01	15.36	15.46	16.56		17.36	18.21
23	Miyanoura	04.45	06.03			08.03	08.43	10.03	10.35	11.18	12.08	13.05	14.03	15.40	15.48	17.00		17.38	18.25
25	Oharamachi	04.48	06.04			08.04	08.44	10.04	10.38	11.19	12.09	13.08	14.04	15.43	15.49	17.03		17.39	18.28
30	A-coop mae	04.52	06.06			08.06	08.46	10.06	10.42	11.21	12.11	13.12	14.06	15.47	15.51	17.07		17.41	18.32
31	Miyanourasho mae	04.54	06.07			08.07	08.47	10.07	10.43	11.22	12.12	13.13	14.07	15.48	15.52	17.08		17.42	18.33
34	Asahimachi	04.57	06.09			08.09	08.49	10.09	10.45	11.24	12.14	13.15	14.09	15.50	15.54	17.10		17.44	18.35
37	Kusugawa	05.01	06.11			08.11	08.51	10.11	10.48	11.26	12.16	13.18	14.11	15.53	15.56	17.13		17.46	18.38
41	Tabugawa	05.04	06.15			08.15	08.55	10.15	10.52	11.30	12.20	13.22	14.15	15.57	16.00	17.17		17.50	18.42
44	Koseda		06.18			08.18	08.58	10.18	10.55	11.33	12.23	13.25	14.18	16.00	16.03	17.22		17.53	18.47
48	Outside airport		06.22			08.22	09.02	10.22	11.00	11.37	12.27	13.30	14.22	16.04	16.07	17.26		17.57	18.52
49	Airport		06.23			08.23	09.03	10.23	11.02	11.38	12.28	13.32	14.23	16.05	16.08	17.27		17.58	18.54
52	Hayasaki		06.25		07.24	08.25	09.05	10.25	11.03	11.40	12.30	13.33	14.25	16.10	16.10	17.32		18.00	18.55
56	Nagakubo		06.28		07.25	08.28	09.08	10.28	11.08	11.43	12.33	13.38	14.28	16.18	16.13	17.40		18.03	19.00
59	Funayuki		06.32		07.29	08.32	09.12	10.32	11.16	11.47	12.37	13.46	14.32	16.19	16.17	17.41		18.07	19.08
62	Gochomae		06.35		07.32	08.35	09.15	10.35	11.17	11.50	12.40	13.47	14.35	16.21	16.22	17.43		18.12	19.09
64	Anbo Port		06.40		07.36	08.39	09.19	10.39	11.19	11.55	12.45	13.49	14.39	16.26	16.26	17.48			19.11
66	Anbo				07.37	08.40	09.20	10.40	11.24	11.57	12.47	13.54	14.40	16.27	16.27	17.49	17.42	18.16	19.16
67	Makino					08.45	09.25	10.45	11.25	11.58	12.48	13.55	14.45	16.33	16.32	17.55		18.17	19.17
68	Museum	05.14				08.53	09.33	10.53	11.31	12.03	12.53	14.01	14.53	16.38	16.40	18.00	17.51	18.22	19.23
78	Hirano					08.54	09.34	10.54	11.36	12.11	13.01	14.06	14.54	16.43	16.41	18.05	17.59	18.30	19.28
85	Mugio					08.56	09.36	10.56	11.41	12.12	13.02	14.11	14.56	16.46	16.43	18.08	18.00	18.31	19.33
86	Botanical Park					09.01	09.41	11.01	11.44	12.14	13.04	14.14	15.01	16.54	16.48	18.16	18.02	18.33	19.36
89	Hara					09.02	09.42	11.02	11.52	12.19	13.09	14.22	15.02	16.59	16.49	18.21	18.07	18.38	19.44
94	Onoaida					09.08	09.48	11.08	11.57	12.20	13.10	14.27	15.08	17.03	16.55		18.08	18.39	19.49
97	JR Hotel			07.22		09.13	09.53			12.26							18.14	18.45	
99	Iwasaki Hotel			07.28		09.18	09.58			12.31							18.19		
102	Koshima			07.33		09.21	10.01			12.36							18.24		
110	Hirauchi			07.38			10.09			12.39							18.26		
114	Yudomari			07.41		09.29	10.14			12.47									
123	Nakama			07.49		09.34	10.18			12.52									
127	Kurio-bashi			07.54															
129	Oko-no-taki											14.31		17.03					

Oko-no-taki – Kurio-bashi – Onoaida – Anbo – Airport – Miyanoura - Nagata

No	Destination	Museum	Nagata	Miyanoura Port	Miyanoura Port	Miyanoura Port	Nagata	Nagata	Miyanoura Port	Nagata	Miyanoura Port	Nagata	Miyanoura Port	Nagata	Miyanoura Port	Nagata	Seaside Hotel	Miyanoura Port
129	Oko-no-raki		06.44	07.59	08.24	09.54			11.00		12.44				15.05			17.45
127	Kurio-bashi		06.49	08.04	08.29	09.59			11.04		12.49				15.09			17.49
123	Nakama		06.57	08.12	08.37	10.07			11.09		12.57		13.39		15.14			17.54
114	Yudomari	04.59	07.00	08.15	08.40	10.10			11.17		13.00		13.44		15.22			18.02
110	Hirauchi	05.01	07.05	08.20	08.45	10.15			11.20		13.05		13.52		15.25			18.05
102	Koshima	05.06	07.10	08.25	08.50	10.20			11.25		13.10		13.55		15.30			18.10
99	Iwasaki Hotel	05.11	07.16	08.31	08.56	10.26			11.30	12.20	13.16		14.00	14.35	15.35	17.00		18.15
97	JR Hotel	05.17	07.17	08.32	08.57	10.27			11.36	12.26	13.17		14.05	14.41	15.41	17.06		18.21
94	Onoaida	05.18	07.22	08.37	09.02	10.32			11.37	12.27	13.22		14.11	14.42	15.42	17.07		18.22
89	Hara	05.23	07.24	08.39	09.04	10.34			11.42	12.32	13.24		14.12	14.47	15.47	17.12		18.27
86	Botanical Park	05.25	07.25	08.40	09.05	10.35			11.44	12.34	13.25		14.17	14.49	15.49	17.14		18.29
85	Mugio	05.26							11.45	12.35			14.19	14.50	15.50	17.15		18.30
78	Hirano	05.34	07.33	08.48	09.13	10.43			11.53	12.43	13.33		14.20	14.58	15.58	17.23		18.38
68	Museum	**05.43**	07.38	08.53	09.18	10.48			11.58	12.48	13.38		14.28	15.03	16.03	17.28	**17.42**	
67	Makino		07.39	08.54	09.19	10.49			11.59	12.49	13.39		14.33	15.04	16.04	17.29	17.47	18.43
66	Anbo					10.52			12.02	12.52	13.42		14.34	15.08	16.08	17.35	17.48	18.44
64	Anbo Port		07.43	08.58	09.23													18.47
62	Gochomae		07.46	09.01	09.26	10.56			12.06	12.56	13.46		14.40	15.11	16.11	17.38	17.52	18.53
59	Funayuki		07.50	09.05	09.30	10.59			12.09	12.59	13.49		14.43	15.15	16.15	17.42	17.55	18.56
56	Nagakubo					11.03			12.13	13.03	13.53		14.47	15.18	16.18	17.45	17.59	19.00
52	Hayasaki		07.53	09.08	09.33	11.06			12.16	13.06	13.56		14.50	15.20	16.20	17.47	18.02	19.03
49	Airport		07.55	09.10	09.35	11.08			12.18	13.08	13.58		14.52	15.21	16.21	17.48	18.04	19.05
48	Outside airport		07.56	09.11	09.36	11.09			12.19	13.09	13.59		14.53	15.25	16.25	17.52	18.08	19.06
44	Koseda		08.00	09.15	09.40	11.13			12.23	13.13	14.03		14.57	15.28	16.28	17.55	18.11	19.10
41	Tabugawa		08.03	09.18	09.43	11.16			12.26	13.16	14.06		15.00	15.32	16.32	17.59	18.15	19.13
37	Kusugawa		08.07	09.22	09.47	11.20		10.37	12.30	13.20	14.10		15.04	15.34	16.34	18.01	18.17	19.17
34	Asahimachi		08.09	09.24	09.49	11.22		10.39	12.32	13.22	14.12		15.06	15.36	16.36	18.03	18.19	19.19
31	Miyanourasho mae		08.11	09.26	09.51	11.24		10.41	12.34	13.24	14.14		15.08	15.37	16.37	18.04	18.20	19.21
30	A-coop mae		08.12	09.27	09.52	11.25		10.42	12.35	13.25	14.15		15.09	15.39	16.39	18.06	18.22	19.22
25	Oharamachi		08.14	09.29	09.54	11.27		10.44	12.37	13.27	14.17		15.11				18.23	19.24
23	Miyanoura		08.15	09.30	09.55	11.28		10.45	12.38	13.28	14.18		15.12	15.40	16.40	18.07	18.25	19.25
21	Port Entrance		08.17	09.32	09.57	11.30	10.05	10.47	12.40	13.30	14.20	12.50	15.14	15.42	16.42	18.09	18.26	19.27
20	Miyanoura Port		08.20	09.35	10.00	11.33	10.09	10.50	12.43	13.33	14.23	12.54	15.17	15.45	16.45	18.12		19.30
17	Futagawa		08.24				10.16	10.54		13.37		13.01		15.49		18.16		
14	Shitoko		08.31				10.21	11.01		13.44		13.06		15.56		18.23		
11	Isso		08.36				10.27	11.06		13.49		13.12		16.01		18.28		
8	Yoshida		08.42					11.12		13.55				16.07		18.34		
4	Inakahama		08.50				10.35	11.20		14.03		13.20		16.15		18.42		
	Nagata		08.52				10.37	11.22		14.05		13.22		16.17		18.44		

Notes: The Museum service (first column) runs March to November only. The Seaside Hotel service runs March to November only.

E. MATSUBANDA CONNECTING BUSES

(FOR THE ARAKAWA TRAIL & SHIRATANI UNSUIKYO)

(Free pass not accepted)

Miyanoura ↔ Yakusugi Museum					
19	Culture Center	04.30	68	Yakusugi museum	17.11
21	Port Entrance	04.31	67	Makino	17.16
22	Noboriagari	04.32	66	Anbo	17.17
23	Miyanoura	04.33	65	Nakaiin mae	17.18
24	Miyanoura shisho	04.34	64	Anbo Port	17.19
25	Oharamachi	04.34	65	Nakaiin mae	17.20
30	Outside A coop	04.35	63	Keisatsusho mae	17.21
31	Miyanourasho mae	04.36	62	Gochomae	17.22
32	Koukou mae	04.37	61	Chuuou	17.22
33	Eidan	04.38	60	Isobe	17.23
34	Asahimachi	04.38	59	Funayuki	17.25
35	Torigoe	04.39	58	Ryuuten	17.26
36	Kusugawa Iriguchi	04.40	57	Kuwano	17.27
37	Kusugawa	04.40	56	Nagakubo	17.28
38	Yunokawa onsen	04.42	49	Airport (Kuukou)	17.33
42	Otokogawa	04.46	48	Outside airport	17.33
43	Nishi Koseda	04.47	46	Shinyoujo mae	17.34
46	Shinyoujo mae	04.50	43	Nishi Koseda	17.37
48	Outside airport	04.51	42	Otokogawa	17.48
49	Airport (Kuukou)		38	Yunokawa onsen	17.42
56	Nagakubo	04.56	37	Kusugawa	17.44
57	Kuwano	04.57	36	Kusugawa Iriguchi	17.44
58	Ryuuten	04.58	35	Torigoe	17.45
59	Funayuki	04.59	34	Asahimachi	17.46
60	Isobe	05.01	33	Eidan	17.46
61	Chuuou	05.02	32	Koukou mae	17.47
62	Gochomae	05.02	31	Miyanourasho mae	17.48
63	Keisatsusho mae	05.03	30	Outside A coop	17.49
65	Nakaiin mae	05.04	25	Oharamachi	17.50
64	Anbo Port	05.05	24	Miyanoura shisho	17.50
65	Nakaiin mae	05.06	23	Miyanoura	17.51
66	Anbo	05.07	22	Noboriagari	17.52
67	Makino	05.08	21	Port Entrance	17.53
68	Yakusugi museum	05.13	19	Culture Center	17.54
			20	Miyanoura Port	17.54

Hirauchi to Yakusugi Museum		
107	Hirauchi iriguchi	04.45
106	Kaminomaki	04.46
101	Yaishi	04.50
100	Iwasaki Hotel	04.51
98	Onoaida onsen	04.51
95	Onoaida chuou	04.52
97	JR Hotel	04.53
95	Onoaida chuou	04.54
94	Onoaida	04.55
93	Futamata gawa	04.55
92	Nakano	04.56
90	Kamiyama	04.59
89	Hara	04.59
88	Hara Iriguchi	05.00
84	Hotogawa	05.03
83	Takahira	05.04
76	Chuuji	05.10
75	Yokomine	05.11
74	Haruta	05.12
73	Morihisajinja mae	05.13
68	Yakusugi Museum	05.18

117

Miyanoura ↔ Anbo

67	Makino	07.20	20	Miyanoura Port	15.40[B]
66	Anbo	07.21	19	Culure Center	15.40
65	Nakaiin mae	07.22	21	Port Entrance	15.41
64	Anbo Port	07.23	22	Noboriagari	15.42
65	Nakaiin mae	07.24	23	Miyanoura	15.43
63	Keisatsusho mae	07.25	24	Miyanoura shisho	15.44
62	Gochomae	07.26	25	Oharamachi	15.44
61	Chuuou	07.26	30	Outside A coop	15.45
60	Isobe	07.27	31	Miyanourasho mae	15.46
59	Funayuki	07.29	32	Koukou mae	15.47
58	Ryuuten	07.30	33	Eidan	15.48
57	Kuwano	07.31	34	Asahimachi	15.48
56	Nagakubo	07.32	35	Torigoe	15.49
49	Airport (Kuukou)	07.37	36	Kusugawa Iriguchi	15.50
48	Outside airport	07.37	37	Kusugawa	15.50
46	Shinryojo mae	07.38	38	Yunokawa onsen	15.52
43	Nishi Koseda	07.41	41	Tabugawa	15.54
42	Otokogawa	07.42	42	Otokogawa	15.56
38	Yunokawa onsen	07.46	43	Nishi Koseda	15.57
37	Kusugawa	07.48	48	Outside airport	16.01
36	Kusugawa Iriguchi	07.48	49	Airport (Kuukou)	16.01
35	Torigoe	07.49	56	Nagakubo	16.06
34	Asahimachi	07.50	57	Kuwano	16.07
33	Eidan	07.50	58	Ryuuten	16.08
32	Koukou mae	07.51	59	Funayuki	16.09
31	Miyanourasho mae	07.52	60	Isobe	16.11
30	Outside A coop	07.53	61	Chuuou	16.12
25	Oharamachi	07.54	62	Gochomae	16.12
24	Miyanoura shisho	07.54	63	Keisatsusho mae	16.13
23	Miyanoura	07.55	65	Nakaiin mae	16.14
22	Noboriagari	07.56	64	Anbo Port	16.15
21	Port Entrance	07.57	65	Nakaiin mae	16.16
19	Culture Center	07.58	66	Anbo	16.17
20	Miyanoura Port	07.58[A]	67	Makino	16.18

[A] and [B] connect with the Matsubanda Shiratani route bus.

Anbo

Miyanoura

Jomon-sugi

Yakushima Airport
Pillow-shaped Lava Field
Koseda
Tabugawa
Kusugawa
Nagamine
Nagakubo
Aiko-dake Trail
Funayuki
Matsumine
Harumaki
Harutahama Beach
Hirano
Botanical Research Park
Takahira
Toroki-no-taki Waterfall
Yamanko Yusi spring
Senpiro-no-taki Waterfall
Mugio
Hara
Onoaida
Sanukawa
Gajumaru Banyan
Bandai-sugi
Mochomu Taro
Mochomu-dake (940)
Koshima
Onoaida Onsen
Hirauchi
Hiirauchi Seaside onsen
Yudomari Seaside onsen
Yudomari
Nakama
Asahi
Nakama Gajumaru
Yakushima Fruit Garden
Kuriohama Beach
Kurio
Tsukasaki tide pool
Natural Mangrove site
Yakushima Youth Travel Village
Oko-no-taki Waterfall
Oko Yusui spring
Shakunage Forest Park
Shichigo-dake (1614)
Janokuchi-taki Waterfall
Eboshi-dake (1488)
Yodogawa Trail Entrance
Onoaida Trail
Yodogawa Hut
Kigen-sugi
Yudomari Trail
Koban-dake (1711)
Hananoego
Ishizuka Hut
Nageshi-dake (1830)
Anbo-dake (1847)
Okina-dake (1860)
Kuromi-dake (1831)
Kurio-dake (1867)
Nagata-dake (1886)
Miyanoura-dake (1935)
Okabu Trail Entrance
Shin-Takatsuka Hut
Takatsuka Hut
Wilson's Stump
Shiratani Unsuikyo
Shiratani Hut
Yayoi-sugi
Aiko-dake (1235)
Taikoiwa Rock
Arakawa Trail Entrance
Tachu-dake (1497)
Yakusugi Land
Arakawa Trail
Yakusugi Museum
Yakushima Island Environmental and Cultural Learning Center
Yakushima World Heritage Center
Kusugawa Onsen
Kusugawa Trail
Kusugawa
Shitogo Gajumaru Park
Shitogo
Fuin-no-taki waterfall
History and Folk Museum
Miyanoura Recreational Park
Isso
Isso Beach
Oura Onsen
Yoshida
Sea turtle center
Yoko valley
Nagata
Nagata Trail
Nagata Inakahama Beach
Nagata Maehama Beach
Yakushima Lighthouse
Seibu Rindo Forest Path
Kuniwari-dake (1323)
Shikanosawa Hut
Shikanosawa Trail
Hananoego Trail

Index

www.ingramcontent.com/pod-product-compliance
Lightning Source LLC
Chambersburg PA
CBHW060438090426
42733CB00011B/2317